# Troubling Violence

# Troubling Violence

## A PERFORMANCE PROJECT

## M. HEATHER CARVER

### AND

## ELAINE J. LAWLESS

UNIVERSITY PRESS OF MISSISSIPPI . . . . . . . . . . . . . . . . . . . *JACKSON*

www.upress.state.ms.us

Designed by Todd Lape

The University Press of Mississippi is a member
of the Association of American University Presses.

∞
Library of Congress Cataloging-in-Publication Data

Carver, M. Heather.
Troubling violence : a performance project / M. Heather Carver and Elaine J. Lawless.
p. cm.
Includes bibliographical references.
ISBN 978-1-60473-208-5 (cloth : alk. paper) 1. Abused women—United States.
2. Family violence—United States. I. Lawless, Elaine J. II. Title.
HV6626.2.C36 2009
362.82'92—dc22                        2008044677

British Library Cataloging-in-Publication Data available

To Ronald P. Carver, Heather's father, and Mary Lago, Elaine's beloved friend, both superb scholars and treasured mentors.

Together, we acknowledge the enormous amount of support and the work, assistance, commitment of time, talent, energy, and passion of the members of the Troubling Violence Performance Project. We also thank the members of the MU Campus Committee against Violence toward Women; psychologist Chrissy Civiletto and social worker Kendra Yoder, who attended our campus performances and helped guide our conversations with troubled audience members; Phebe Lauffer, fiscal officer in Theatre; Kim Ryan, a local minister; our colleague, Kitty Holland; and all of our friends in women's and gender studies, English, and the Theatre Department. Additional thanks go to to the Center for Arts and Humanities, the MU Office of Research, and the dean of Arts and Sciences at the University of Missouri. We are grateful to the University Press of Mississippi and particularly to editor Craig Gill for his patience and guidance. We thank our families; our incredibly supportive spouses, Bill Horner and Sandy Rikoon, and our daughters for the time and energy given to our work on the troupe and this book. Special thanks go to Ronald and Mary Louise Carver and Bob and Judy Horner for their support in the early days of the troupe, when Tricia and Ellie were so young. And we acknowledge the shoulders of the women who have supported us through their feminist work. We thank all of our mothers, sisters, and daughters, for whom these stories must continue to be told. We are grateful for the invitations to perform for MU classes, groups, other university campuses, churches, shelters, and community venues across the United States. Most of all, we thank all the women and men who have shared their stories with us for the work of the troupe. The telling and retelling and the sharing of your stories continues to make a difference by providing hope and inspiration for others.

# Playbill

## The Troubling Violence Performance Project

### ORIGINAL CAST (2003)

Constance Bailey

Heather Carver

Sadie Chandler

Patricia Downey

Brock Fisher

Shelley Ingram

Kate Berneking Kogut

Elaine Lawless

### PLAYERS (2003–2008)

Heidi Arni

Santana Dempsy

Marlys Johnson

Stephanie Koehler

Elyse Link

Lisa Lynch

Whit Loy

Cece McFarland

Molly McFatrich

Andréa Onstad

Josh Pfeffercorn

Emilie Sabath

Matt Salzberg

Struby

Brandy Taylor

Kari Winkelmeyer

Trevor Wise

# The Troubling Violence Performance Project

Artistic Director . . . . . . . . . . . . . . . . . . . . . . . . . . . . . M. Heather Carver
Producer . . . . . . . . . . . . . . . . . . . . . . . . . . . . . . . . . . . . Elaine J. Lawless

The Troubling Violence Performance Project (TVPP) emerged out of a cross-disciplinary interest between Heather Carver (performance studies) and Elaine Lawless (folklore studies). Carver and Lawless met in 2001, soon after Lawless had published her ethnography of a shelter for battered women. They began talking about their shared interest in studying narrative, ethnography, and performance. They then decided to begin the project by forming a troupe that would perform the narratives in Lawless's 2001 book, *Women Escaping Violence: Empowerment through Narrative*. As the artistic director, Carver adapted the narratives from the book. She also invited troupe members to share their own stories or stories given to them by others who had experienced abuse. Carver then worked with each student on his/her performance.

When the troupe began in the fall of 2003, graduate students in both the English and Theatre Departments were invited to join as performers. The troupe first performed for the University of Missouri Task Force against Partnership Violence, then performed more than thirty times that year—for the law school, political science courses, women's studies courses, local church and community groups, current residents of women's shelters, and the women's center. The troupe also did a series of performances for the MU Athletic Department, coaching staff, and student athletes and traveled to several scholarly conferences to perform. The troupe continues to perform at a wide variety of venues every year. We invite a professional counselor/therapist to every performance to facilitate questions and provide support for audience members in crisis.

Every performance of TVPP has elicited an overwhelming response from the audience, and following performances, women often volunteer to give their own stories to the troupe for future performances. The troupe now performs more stories from people in the community than stories from Lawless's work. And the troupe has continued to grow. We have had approximately fifteen students involved, both graduate and undergraduate. They are performing stories that are relevant to our audiences—stories from students, university faculty and staff, and members of the community.

# Contents

The Pre-Show . . . . . . . . . . . . . . . . . . . . . . . . . . . . . . . . . . . . . . . . . . . . . . . . . . . 3
Backdrop . . . . . . . . . . . . . . . . . . . . . . . . . . . . . . . . . . . . . . . . . . . . . . . . . . . . . 16

## Act I

The Academic Stage . . . . . . . . . . . . . . . . . . . . . . . . . . . . . . . . . . . . . . . . . . . 21
Character Development . . . . . . . . . . . . . . . . . . . . . . . . . . . . . . . . . . . . . . . . 29
First Run . . . . . . . . . . . . . . . . . . . . . . . . . . . . . . . . . . . . . . . . . . . . . . . . . . . . . 35
Breaking the Fourth Wall . . . . . . . . . . . . . . . . . . . . . . . . . . . . . . . . . . . . . 44
Performing Violence . . . . . . . . . . . . . . . . . . . . . . . . . . . . . . . . . . . . . . . . . . 60

## Act II

Writing the Body . . . . . . . . . . . . . . . . . . . . . . . . . . . . . . . . . . . . . . . . . . . . 105
Violence against Our Bodies . . . . . . . . . . . . . . . . . . . . . . . . . . . . . . . . . 107
Violence at Home . . . . . . . . . . . . . . . . . . . . . . . . . . . . . . . . . . . . . . . . . . . 116
Curtain Call . . . . . . . . . . . . . . . . . . . . . . . . . . . . . . . . . . . . . . . . . . . . . . . . 132
A Courtroom Scene . . . . . . . . . . . . . . . . . . . . . . . . . . . . . . . . . . . . . . . . . 135
A Conference Scene . . . . . . . . . . . . . . . . . . . . . . . . . . . . . . . . . . . . . . . . . 142
Life, with No Chance . . . . . . . . . . . . . . . . . . . . . . . . . . . . . . . . . . . . . . . . 145

Bibliography . . . . . . . . . . . . . . . . . . . . . . . . . . . . . . . . . . . . . . . . . . . . . . . . 151

# Troubling Violence

# The Pre-Show

*Lights up on center stage. Two women sit at a small table with an umbrella. HEATHER and ELAINE write in notebooks. One has long curly auburn hair and short sleeves, and the other is covered from head to toe in sun-protective clothing and a wide-brimmed sun hat. Soft tropical tunes play in the background; lights indicate water waving behind them. The woman in the hat directly addresses the audience.*

**HEATHER** *(looking up from her notebook)* This book is about the journey that we have taken together to challenge violence against women in their homes. We formed the Troubling Violence Performance Project to introduce a way of communicating about the complexities of intimate partner violence. We have continually been intrigued by the ways in which our academic disciplines—folklore and performance studies—have spoken to each other through our personal, scholarly, and artistic endeavors as we tell the story of the Troubling Violence Performance Project. Some of the tale is revealed through memory and some through recording, while other projects unfold during the performing itself. We draw on autoethnography and performative writing to chart our paths backward and forward in time, for while the troupe and our work have occurred over the course of five years, we and the women whose stories we tell spread out into decades of life experience.

Maybe we should begin where we are. Here. Together. Elaine and I write our story of the troupe every day. The trick is to find the time to catch up with ourselves. So we've taken a couple of days away from our "normal" lives to focus and go where our feet have never taken us before. A pedicure. This simple idea that probably extends through time—the care and nurturing of our feet—is foreign to us. Elaine's feet take her to her academic jobs, to her national conventions, and for three decades to her three children's softball, basketball, and soccer games, their tae kwon do, gymnastics, and diving. My feet have been trying to keep up with two small children, an emerging academic career, and most recently intense treatment for breast cancer.

So we take our feet to this serene lake environment where we feel awkward as someone else begins to help take care of the bunions, the soreness, and the neglect of our literal soles.

And we begin. Here. Thinking of you, our audience, as we share the story in the now.

Reflecting, we decide that to tell the story of the troupe in linear fashion would be to deny the work's multiple and circular patterns. The narrative of the narrative loops in and out of times, dates, and places. We seek to provide more of a holistic experience for you, dear audience, as we discover and acknowledge the footsteps and the landscape of the terrain of this work.

*The woman with the auburn hair stands up, notebook in hand, and walks downstage, addressing the audience.*

ELAINE   In truth, I had applied for the sixteen-week Writing across the Curriculum for Faculty Seminar for the extra money. Jess and Kate were expensive propositions with their summer camps and uniforms for gymnastics, soccer, basketball, track, and cheerleading. The shoes—pairs and pairs and pairs of shoes, each a little different for each sport—the trips, the bags (each a little different, then discarded to the back of the closet). Today's extracurricular kid costs lots of money. Shell out the cash, or your kid does not get all the necessary opportunities for his or her growth. Our kids should be giants! So I did it for the extra bucks.

After all, I had begun my career at MU in the early 1980s with a first-year salary of $19,500, with a Ph.D., several publications, and a year's teaching under my belt.

This was rather simple, I had thought. But the $2,500 stipend shrank by one-third as it appeared on my pay stub. Hardly worth it, I had begun to think as I sat bored and wondering what else I could be doing with my time on Thursday afternoons. Little did I know that this faculty gathering would change the course of my career, my life, my writing, my teaching, how I did my research. How could I have known that one of the strangers sitting across the table from me, equally smashed between faculty on both sides at the immense table that first day, would become more than a colleague, more than a friend—a collaborator, a small miracle.

**HEATHER**   Perhaps I didn't even notice her the first day.

**ELAINE**   I was feeling awkward because I was one of the "experienced" faculty, meaning faculty who had been included in the seminar because of the experiences we could bring to the discussions based on the fact that we had been offering writing-intensive courses for years.

**HEATHER**   Be honest.

**ELAINE**   OK, I also did these writing-intensive courses for the guarantee of smaller classes and a teaching or grading assistant. Made good sense to me; I had always had my students write a lot anyway, so I got with the program. Thus, I was there as one of the program's poster children. I would have to sacrifice one day per week for the duration of the seminar in exchange for cold, hard cash. I looked around the table and half-listened as the others introduced themselves—math, political science, communications, physics, philosophy.

**HEATHER**   Theatre.

**ELAINE**   The philosopher was sitting next to me on one side, the math genius on the other. Neither believed in smiling, apparently. I was acquainted with the woman across the table who always seemed to be on the make. I smiled to myself as she spoke in a trained low, husky voice and flipped her long hair off her shoulders at appropriate intervals. Her eyes were dark with makeup and her lips red and full. I began to believe I just might not make it past the first meeting. But the woman from the Theatre Department, Heather Carver—

**HEATHER** sat at the end of the table—

**ELAINE** —a tall, imposing woman, obvious even as she sat at the table, towering over the heads of those jammed next to her.

**HEATHER** She had a bright, open face and an honest, loud laugh—

**ELAINE** In fact, I jealously wondered, What *were* they laughing about down there at her end of the table?

**HEATHER** Did we walk out of that first meeting together, chatting about our courses and our "assignments" for the seminar?

**ELAINE** Or did we talk the second or even the third meeting? At this point, I'm not sure. But, clearly, we did begin to talk and share syllabi—

**HEATHER** and bibliographies, and books we were reading and how we used writing in our classrooms.

**ELAINE** Over the course of that seminar, my world opened up for the first time in twenty years. I was talking with a colleague about my life, my work, my teaching, and we had real conversations that lasted past the time we were supposed to pick up our kids, past the seminar boundaries, past requirements, and into a new, uncharted territory. Had she, too, perceived a kindred spirit in me?

**HEATHER** We began to meet and share ideas, our books, research, the politics of our departments, our children, our careers, our lives.

**ELAINE** We met on campus. We met in restaurants. I went to her home and talked with her as her small children slept and as she nursed her youngest daughter. I had two daughters, too, I told her. Our conversations were sprinkled with politics—

**HEATHER** research—

**ELAINE** budding teeth, cheerleading—

**HEATHER** injuries on the basketball court—

ELAINE   reading skills—

HEATHER   Ellie's birth—

ELAINE   my son in California, my disastrous first marriage. We shared our research interests and our training in ethnography from very different academic centers.

HEATHER   We marveled together about the partners we had both chosen, amazing, smart men who were supportive, cooperative, real partners in parenting, careers, homemaking, cooking.

ELAINE   She told me about her husband's cancer and the wonders of her daughters' births; I told her about the adoption of our younger daughter, Kate, and about Kate's own demons caused by being abandoned by her birth mother.

HEATHER   I told Elaine about performative writing—

ELAINE   and I told Heather about ethnographic writing.

HEATHER   I shared the difficulties of working in Texas with the narratives of women with HIV and AIDS and my concerns about women's physical and mental health and the power of narrative to share women's experiences.

ELAINE   I told her about my years of ethnographic research in a battered women's shelter and the study of women's narratives that came out of that work.

ELAINE AND HEATHER (in unison)   We read each other's papers.

HEATHER   We talked for long afternoon hours, trying to sandwich our conversations between all the other demands on our selves— squeezing time for each other from schedules already bulging with department demands—

ELAINE   our families, our writing, our reading, our teaching—

HEATHER   our work with graduate students.

**ELAINE**  We shared books, exercise plans, and the pain of family deaths—

**HEATHER**  names of good therapists, and hugs.

**ELAINE**  In addition to all of this, I marveled to see that Heather could also balance going to the theater night after night for rehearsals and productions, stay past midnight, and still arrive fresh on the scene the next morning. Her drive and enthusiasm were contagious.

**HEATHER** *(laughs)*  I'd found my match.

**ELAINE**  I, too, was a woman in superdrive. We might not slow each other down; in fact, the opposite has occurred. We seem to be challenging the academic universe—

**HEATHER**  but at least now each of us has a partner for the journey.

*Elaine moves downstage and directly addresses the audience—trying to make eye contact with someone nodding knowingly in the second row.*

**ELAINE**  In recent years, I have come to believe in synchronicity. Not fate, but synchronicity, that there are moments in our lives when the potential for things to come together is ripe with possibility— because we are eager, ready, desperate, perhaps. Synchronicity is not the evidence of forethought or planning, but it is the seed of desire. There are pregnant moments when aspects of possibility hang in the air. We probably miss thousands of these rich moments simply because we are not watching carefully or because they slip by silently and too quickly, or because we are so busy with all the small stuff we have decided is important that we have our noses to the ground and cannot see the moments when they arrive. We miss the flicker of recognition and, blink, it's gone.

But occasionally, I suppose, if we are living right and our desire is great enough (meaning the lack is so profound that we are at least tuned to the possibility of seeing, or hearing, or touching the flicker and recognizing it for what it is), we get lucky. Ineffable as this sounds (perhaps preposterous, even), I do actually believe it can happen. This is exactly how I met my second husband. Broke and broken, freshly wounded by a brutal marriage and a horrendous divorce, mother to a beautiful son I nearly lost, I moved to Bloomington as a new graduate student. I was sent to the Folklore Archives at Indiana University to find Sandy, the student director. "She" did not seem to be around; I was irritated. But a soft-spoken, bearded, balding man in rolled blue jeans and a red flannel shirt peered around the shelving units to claim quietly that he was, in fact, Sandy. One of those miracle moments. I have been with him now for nearly thirty years, raising my son and our daughter and adopting with him another child because home, family, and children were all parts of a dream we shared from the beginning. Synchronicity.

I shared that story with Heather, too, as I told her I felt our own meeting was somewhere in that same miraculous neighborhood. Life at the university had not mirrored my present family life. Twenty-five years had yielded only fleeting possible moments for rich collegial relationships. For years, I would force myself to make lists of my "friends" in my journals, just to put names down on paper as physical evidence that I had actually met some human beings with whom I could connect on personal grounds. Gradually, I actually did have a few good friends—soul mates, in fact—but mostly they were older women who were my mentors, my support system, my own cheerleaders, and former participants in some of my field research. But I could always count them all on one hand.

**HEATHER** We laughed a great deal.

**ELAINE AND HEATHER** We talked over one another—

**ELAINE** each more excited—

**HEATHER** trying to claim the limited space for our conversations.

**ELAINE** Yet we could sense, too, when we ought to be more quiet and provide some space for the other to struggle with ideas, thoughts, approaches, propositions, ways to word a sentence, convince a colleague of our deeply felt convictions, our passions, and how to provide for the legitimate needs of our graduate students.

HEATHER   Orality—

ELAINE   ethnography—

HEATHER   oral interpretation—

ELAINE   performance—

HEATHER   verbal art—

ELAINE   the power of narrative. We share a common language even though we come to this core from two different disciplines—folklore and communication.

HEATHER   We read each other's writing, our voices loud, excited as we make connections—

ELAINE   move into new territory, challenge each other to do something new.

HEATHER   Why don't we start a performance troupe of students and have them memorize some of the stories from your book? We could offer performances with discussions following to a wide range of campus and community groups.

ELAINE   I'm stunned. I want to hear more. How might this work? What, exactly, do you have in mind—a play? A skit? I knew the narrators in my book intimately. I had carried their voices around in my head for nearly five years, since I first tape-recorded them in a damp, dim back room of the shelter with only empty boxes, torn Christmas decorations, worn stuffed animals, and two folding chairs.

HEATHER   No, no, not a play, and certainly not a skit.

ELAINE   Heather was so excited she could hardly slow down enough to explain.

**HEATHER**   Our students will tell the stories they choose from your book. Three, four, even five of them would each tell a different story, one after the other, performing monologues.

**ELAINE**   No stage, no props, no costumes?

**HEATHER**   Right! Only a woman and her voice, her story. After the stories have been performed, we will regroup with the audience and discuss the stories and ask the audience how they responded, ask them what they want to talk about. Just like the HIV stories I worked with in Texas, these are taboo stories in our culture because the subjects—AIDS and domestic violence—are taboo subjects, particularly for women. We do not have forums for these topics. They are our dirty little secrets. We get the stories out, then we talk about them with the audience.

**ELAINE**   "Reperformance," I thought, telling the stories of the women from the shelter. I knew I wanted to do more with this material, with these women's stories, after I published the book, but what? Field research, ethnographic writing, scholarly articles, university press books. This is the world I knew and had become comfortable in, just because I had managed to do it! But I'd done that, been there. I knew I wanted to try something imaginative and new. Intrigued, I longed for more.

**HEATHER**   We talked and talked.

**ELAINE**   We painted the picture of the troupe in the air that surrounded our heads, our bodies, our minds.

**HEATHER**   It began to take shape.

**ELAINE**   We agreed to "trouble" violence in ways that had never before been offered.

**HEATHER**   We would tell the stories, expose the lies, the danger, the fear, the secrets.

**ELAINE**   Telling would be exposing.

**HEATHER**   The stories would be real, never fabricated fictions—

**ELAINE**   only actual stories from the women I had known—poured from the mouths of our own students to audiences eager to know the truth.

**HEATHER**   And we would engage our audiences.

**ELAINE**   We would provide a safe space for other women to hear these stories and relate them to their own lives—

**HEATHER**   the lives of their daughters, sisters, friends, mothers, and grandmothers.

**ELAINE**   We would perform the stories, then wait.

**HEATHER**   I can wait forever. We will not go into these presentations with a set agenda of questions to ask.

**ELAINE**   We will wait to see what the audience wants and needs to talk about.

**HEATHER**   We will wait until they speak.

**ELAINE**   And if they want to share their own stories, we will all listen.

**HEATHER**   This will be a safe space for talk; sharing will be entirely motivated by the audience.

**ELAINE**   We want and need to hear what affects and empowers *them.*

**HEATHER**   And then we need to write about it, performatively.

*The two women return to the table, deep in thought. Beat.*

**ELAINE** *(looking up, confused)*   But what *is* performative writing?

**HEATHER** *(laughing)*   Stay with me; we're already doing it. Maybe this will help. Actually, I've always said that performative writing is embodied writing. Academic writing often must focus as a response to others' ideas; performative writing dances into new territory.

*Heather opens a copy of* The Green Window, *essays from the performative writing conference in 2001, and begins to read.*

**HEATHER**   My colleague in communication and performance studies, Fred Corey, says performative writing is "a contemporary smile that is intriguing, alluring, wearisome, and provocative. No one definition of performative writing can or will exist; the elusive nature of the phrase is a component of its value. If a clear definition existed, if an understanding of the phrase were right or wrong, if a noted scholar authored the final characteristic of the concept, performative writing may well be put to a deserved rest" (Miller and Pelias 2001, xii).

*Heather hands the book to Elaine, who reads aloud a quotation from Lesa Lockford.*

**HEATHER**   "Performative writing expands the purview of the scholarly endeavor, which at its most basic impulse is to tell the human story of our world" (Miller and Pelias 2001, xii).

*Elaine gets excited and begins to read another definition from Tami Spry.*

**ELAINE**   Listen to this. "Performative writing composes the body into being. Such a praxis requires that my performing body believe in language's representational ability, thus putting my body at (the) stake, both burning and lighting the linguistic match, collapsing the boundaries between these (f)acts" (Miller and Pelias 2001, ix).

*Heather is nodding enthusiastically as she realizes Elaine is beginning to understand the process. They begin sharing lines from Jonathan Gray's definitions of performative writing.*

**HEATHER**  Performative writing is "a recognition of the ability of words of the page to perform and an attempt to write in such a way that draws attention to that performance . . . a strategy of discursive production that turns against its tendencies to sediment meaning and shape perceptions; a language that acknowledges its ability to do so" (Miller and Pelias 2001, viii).

**ELAINE**  "A blend of genres and a rupturing of boundaries; a carnival through the streets that borrows from everything it meets. Sometimes it is a funeral procession. Sometimes it is New Orleans."

**HEATHER**  How amazing that he said that before Katrina. *(Beat)*.
 Then he says that performative writing is "a new name for possibly new combinations of creative nonfiction writing strategies that are *not* new."

**ELAINE**  "A form of writing desperately clinging to the embodiment of an utterance: look, a body was here!"

**HEATHER**  "A form of writing eager to mirror performance patterns—ritual especially, but others as well."

**ELAINE**  "A call for the celebration of aesthetic writing as scholarly writing; a critique of the norms of academic writing."
 Wow.

*Beat.*

**HEATHER**  "A sensuous reporting of observations external and internal, but mostly where such distinctions collapse into one another."

**ELAINE**  "A lie; a joke; a tall tale; a conflation; an exaggeration; a series of strategic elisions; narratives that are unabashedly deceptive and brutally honest."

**HEATHER**  "An excuse to laugh,"

**ELAINE AND HEATHER** *(together)* "an opportunity to cry." (Gray, Miller and Pelias 2001, viii)

*Beat.*

**HEATHER**   You know, everything we're doing here reminds me of what Lynn Miller and Ron Pelias have always claimed—that performative writing is "where the body and the spoken word, performance practice and theory, the personal and the scholarly, come together" (2001, v).

*The two women resume their seats at the table, take out their notebooks and pens, and begin to write.*

# Backdrop

This book is about violence. It is about the way we have researched partnership violence and learned to recognize the pain of abuse in the eyes of women in every sector of our lives. We see it in the eyes of our students, our mothers, our sisters, our friends.

Together we have formed a performance troupe that travels to venues in the campus and in the community, to conferences and retreat centers. All the performers in this troupe are students who work with us in our academic worlds. They perform monologues, stories of women and men who live with and escape from pain, abuse, and violence. The more we do this work, the more women come forward and give us the gift of their stories for the work of the troupe.

We never conceived of this performance project as entertainment. There is no set for our stories, no props, no programs, no costumes. We come as we are, women and men from everyday walks of life ready to tell our stories and those that belong to others who live among us.

The narrative performances are a vehicle. They serve to bring violence and abuse into the room. In this safe space we have created, we ask the audience to listen and acknowledge that the dangers are real, the pain absolute, the survival awe-inspiring.

We tell the stories, and then we wait, quietly and patiently, asking the audience to join us in serious contemplation and discussion.

What have they heard in these stories? The performances *never* fail to elicit thoughtful responses; audience members speak with hesitation at first, noting how the stories made them feel. They ask the performers about the stories they just told. They want to know if the stories are those of the performers themselves. This seems to make a difference to the audience. Sometimes the performers *are* telling their own stories; sometimes they confess that the story they told was their own. Sometimes they defer.

Sometimes they explain how they came to have and perform a particular story. The audience asks the performers how they feel telling these stories. And, gradually, audience members begin to open up and offer their own stories, their own experiences of violence, the experiences of their sisters, their friends. Sometimes their voices crack with emotion; sometimes they cannot speak. Sometimes they weep openly; sometimes they work hard to hold back the tears. We have done our work well when we break the taboo and expose the shame that surrounds our cultural responses to violence in the home, in our most intimate relationships with people we love and who beat us and bring us down.

Perhaps no other topic carries with it more shame, more confusion, more suffering than violence against our bodies and our minds by men who say they love us. We blame ourselves for his rages; we hide our bruises and our broken bones; we lie to doctors, nurses, and therapists; we cover for him; we stay with him "for the sake of the children" and in doing so lose our selves. We are the walking wounded, and we are everywhere.

This book is about recognizing what it means to look out at an audience of thirty people and *know* without a doubt that more than half—*more than half*—of the women in that room know firsthand what it feels like to be hit in the face, kicked in the stomach, pushed, held down, choked, put down, berated, demeaned, and made to feel unworthy, dispensable, invisible.

We invite you into the world of the Troubling Violence Performance Project.

We invite you to "trouble" with us the intimate violence.

We invite you to challenge with us the cultural frames that endorse male *entitlement*.

Together we can erase the shame, out the violence, and identify alternatives to women who find themselves surprised by violence.

We do *not* have to accept violence as a way of life; we can expect better. There are ways to change the culture and refuse the role of victim.

# Act I

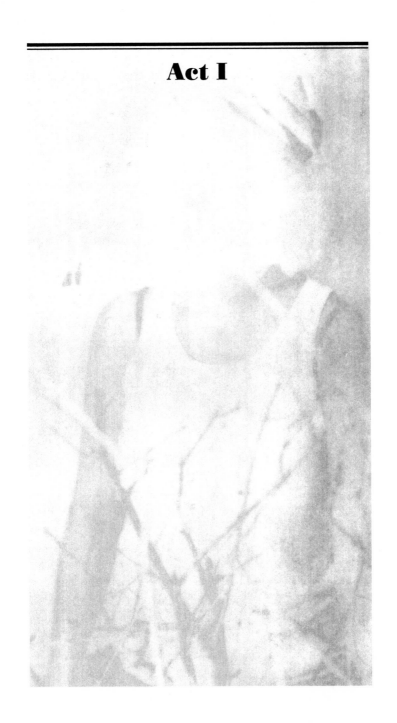

# The Academic Stage

ELAINE *rises from her seat and begins to talk directly to the audience.*
*She comfortably shares her notes as though she knows each audience*
*member, directly addressing them.*

ELAINE  Unless we take a different approach to our ethnographic
projects in the fields of folklore and anthropology, it is quite possible
that we will continue to reinvent the wheel, so to speak, and find
ourselves creating wider and wider circles in the sand. Since James
Clifford and George Marcus and Ruth Behar and Deborah Gordon
created new guideposts for the work of ethnography as well as how
we might better "write culture," we have attempted to refine some
of their main points by this method or that without actually offering new evidence about how to improve on the enterprise. We have
certainly become more cognizant of the pitfalls, dangers, and mis-
constructions that are possible whenever we embark on an endeavor
that attempts to study, understand, and represent the Other or the
Self. The first holds within its core the possibility and probability
of romanticizing, exoticizing, and colonizing the Other; the latter
claims the space too near to narcissism, egoism, and denial to be
a comfortable space for most of us. Many graduate students can
theorize eloquently about the process of ethnographic endeavors yet
cannot write their own ethnographies differently because the process
becomes too complicated by the vagaries of the "doing" of it—both
in the field research, as the students locate themselves within a field
situation, and in the writing of the ethnography, where every word
becomes loaded and potentially offensive in one way or another.
Some desert the discipline altogether; others blunder through
and finish deeply dissatisfied with what they have wrought. A few,
including myself, maintain a steadfast allegiance to the ethnographic

project but move variously through moments of feeling paralyzed as well as moments of true epiphany.

Perhaps one of the primary reasons we may feel as though our thinking in regard to ethnography and ethnographic writing has not progressed much in the past decade or two is that folklorists, like scholars and practitioners in other disciplines, can be too closely bound up in the scholarship and thinking of their own disciplines. Cross-disciplinary and interdisciplinary work is absolutely essential for us to break free of the constraints of our own thinking and practice. Folklorists copiously read and cite other folklorists, quite often cite anthropologists, occasionally cite sociologists, only rarely cite creative nonfiction writers, and less occasionally cite communication and performance studies scholars, writers, and practitioners. Conversely, scholars in many of these obviously "allied disciplines" seem not to have ever heard of folklore studies and have no clue about how closely their work parallels ours. For example, in her experimental 2004 textbook/novel, *The Ethnographic I* (2004), Carolyn Ellis, a prolific writer and scholar in the field of "autoethnography" within the field of communication, gives a brief summary of her subfield by giving the history of qualitative research, quoting mostly sociologists and noting the emergence of "grounded theory" and then moving to the influence of the "ethnography of communication." Most folklorists will have the same reaction I had to one particular paragraph in Ellis's book—utter amazement. Ellis offers this history in answer to a hypothetical question from a graduate student in a seminar: What is the role of qualitative inquiry in the rest of communication scholarship?

> "We can trace some roots to the ethnography of communication (also called the ethnography of speaking) literature of the 1960s and 1970s," I respond, "which emphasized rules for communicating, both verbally and nonverbally. Gerry Philipsen, for example, wrote 'Speaking "like a Man" in Teamsterville' in 1975. Through participant observation and interviews, he studied how blue-collar, low-income, white males valued

speaking 'like a man' and how they learned implicit rules. . . .
Philipsen wrote traditional ethnographic prose, emphasizing
patterns of speaking. His students, such as Donal Carbaugh
and Tamar Katriel, have continued doing ethnographies of
speaking." (12)

Ellis then goes on to describe some "interpretive" ethnographic
studies in communication in the 1970s and 1980s, including Tom
Benson's "Another Shootout in Cowtown," a story complete with
"scenes and dialogue, and Michael Pacanowsky's "Slouching towards
Chicago," a dramatic piece about academic practices, particularly
presenting papers at academic conferences.

In answer to another hypothetical question from a student,
"Have other areas in communication also picked up on
ethnography?" Ellis responds, "Yes. Ethnographic and interview
studies now are prevalent in organizational, media, performance, and
health communication studies" (12).

My discomfort with her "history" here is heightened by her
bibliography: Dell Hymes, Joel Shertzer, and Richard Bauman
appear nowhere. Granted, hers is a book about autoethnography
as it has emerged in the field of communication, but to even offer a
*brief* history of the "ethnography of communication" and not mention
sociolinguistics and anthropological and folklore studies that have
emerged in full force over the past thirty-plus years seems to me
to be a blatant example of the isolation of academic disciplines.
Even though I do not see folklorists going very far afield, I can say
unequivocally that folklorists go beyond folklore scholarship more
than scholars in other disciplines seem to venture. In the case of
ethnography within the field of communication, there certainly
exists a chasm, a void, of knowledge about what other fields are
doing that corresponds in substance and form with the efforts of
scholars such as Ellis. In fact, it is sobering to see the advertisements
for a new book series in "Ethnographic Alternatives," edited by Ellis
and Arthur Bochner, that includes nearly twenty volumes to date but
not one by an anthropologist or folklorist.

Conversely, I find Ellis's "novelistic textbook" a delightful approach to pedagogy, and I think the evolution of autoethnography provides a significant next step past Clifford and Marcus's reflexive anthropology. Perhaps Ellis does not quite convince the reader that her work is neither narcissistic nor more literary than ethnographic, but she hits the mark with her arguments about how scrutiny of the self in its interactions with others is important in understanding both ourselves and others. I think she is correct in assuming that there is no Other beyond the Other that interacts with our own Self. That is, Others and Selves are created only through their interactions, and paying attention to those interactions lies at the heart of understanding what transpires between human beings.

**HEATHER** At this juncture, our work in folklore and theater/performance studies enters this unfolding picture of cross-disciplinary thinking and work. We have been working together to identify the intersections of performance studies and folklore studies as they have emerged in the twenty-first century. My training is based solidly in the Northwestern school of performance studies that identifies closely with Dwight Conquergood and the performance approach that grew directly out of the oral interpretation of literature but expanded into arenas of performances of the Self and the Other. I teach courses in autobiography and autoethnography as well as other performance studies courses within the Department of Theatre at Missouri. I was hired specifically to bring these aspects to a more traditional theater department that teaches acting, playwriting, and theater production.

**ELAINE** My work and that of my teachers is closely aligned in many ways with the emergence in the 1960s and 1970s of the ethnography of communication/speaking "performance-centered" school of sociolinguists that influenced folklore studies. While performance studies students and scholars may not cite folklorists, some do acknowledge this history with Dell Hymes, Joel Shertzer, Richard Bauman, and Clifford Geertz, noting the intersections between sociolinguistic performance theory and a new thrust in communication studies that grew out of oral interpretation. Performance studies scholars note the importance of the world of orality, both in context and in performance.

Perhaps here is a good place to note how the "ethnography of speaking" led to the emergence of "performance centered folkloristics" that revolutionized the study of folk culture—moving the discipline from the study of static texts to one that identifies texts within context and, more importantly, recognizes the continuative components of each "performance" of a text as performative, dynamic, and unique. This newly conceived performance approach to the study of traditional culture applies not only to the production of oral narratives within identifiable "folk groups" but also to processes as diverse as chair making and religious ritual, dance, and belief. The intersections between the disciplines of performance studies and folklore studies should be apparent: they utilize similar languages to explore the inherent processes of similar kinds of cultural exigencies. Yet we are quite confident when we state that neither discipline has utilized the thinking and writing of the other discipline in ways adequate to the task of creating a new arena for intellectual and pragmatic discussion.

There are certainly folklorists in departments of performance studies—such as Barbara Kirshenblatt-Gimblett's position at the Tisch School for the Performing Arts. Yet her situation seems quite rare, and rarely do we find folklorists at home in communication departments. It is heartening to see that the American Folklore Society now has a creative writing and folklore section, where folklorists share their creative writing, trying to find new models for their personal encounters with ethnographic field research.

**HEATHER** We are happy to see folklorists quoting Conquergood and performance studies scholars using Bauman's work on performance. And we know and acknowledge the work of Rhodessa Jones, Moises Kaufman, D. Soyini Madison, E. Patrick Johnson, Olorisa Omi Osun Olomo (Joni L. Jones), Terry Galloway and Donna Nudd, and Anna Deavere Smith, and other ethnographic performers who take us beyond entertainment into the arena of human rights and social justice.

ELAINE   In folklore, we learn as well from those who seek to use creative or literary nonfiction in their writing about folklore and ethnography, including Margaret Yocum, Jo Radner, and Amy Skill-man, who founded the new creative writing section of the American Folklore Society.

HEATHER   We like the way artists accomplish things in teams—in groups. Performance demands collaboration. The academy too often praises and rewards scholars, relying more on an archaic "great man" model of independence, ego—

ELAINE   the "solo" book publication.

HEATHER   How does the collaboration and editorship get rewarded?

ELAINE   It often doesn't.

HEATHER   I'm thinking of Soyini Madison and Judith Hamera's impressive handbook of performance studies, which offers conversations from across the field of performance studies—from politics of location to performance of ethnography and beyond.

ELAINE   And there I see the names of folklorists—finally.

HEATHER   But doesn't it make you wonder? This five-hundred-page book—What rewards exist in academic positions for this kind of collaborative work? Do edited volumes get full credit?

ELAINE   I'm on the campus promotion and tenure committee. I can answer that question with an emphatic "No." They don't count as much; they are discredited.

HEATHER   I was told in my third-year review meeting that my edited volume with two other women scholars was "fine," but I still needed a sole-authored book for tenure.

**ELAINE**  As nonscientists, we regularly face the judgmental nature and outright distain of our collaborative work. If we are working together, does our research count?

**HEATHER**  If we had a laboratory, would our collaboration make more sense to others? Do we need to use terms like *primary investigator*? How would we determine that anyway?

**ELAINE**  Scientific research team? Multiple authors on a published article? Percentage of effort?

**HEATHER**  Elaine and I have discovered that ethnography informs performance through a careful focus on the real stories of women's lives. We can perform real-life stories that have been given to us by abused women as a means of sharing, analyzing, understanding, learning, and teaching about intimate partner violence. A fictional series of performances lacks the true-life story's power of the *real*—the right now, here, togetherness, in this moment—nature of the personal intimate narrative.

Feminist ethnographic performance moves narratives into a safe space of open communication. We extend the feminist gathering, collecting, and writing about the culture of violence into performance spaces as a means of empowering women and lessening the culture of violent men's entitlement that surrounds our everyday lives.

How does performance inform the ethnographic project? Performance studies has turned the traditional theatrical focus of the actor on stage into a multilayered dialogic performance involving performers, stories, and listeners. The locus of control is jarred, shaken, moved, and dismantled in the process.

When we perform the stories in our troupe, we make ourselves open to the moment and time of the performance (the first performance by a woman narrating her own story and our reperformance in a performance space with a different audience). The troupe members perform a wide variety of narratives—each member who is present rises out of the audience to tell her story and then returns to her seat when she finishes, both literally and figuratively being the "girl next door" who faces violence on a daily basis or any woman in the audience. After the troupe members perform, we and all of the performers gather in front in a semicircle and ask the audience to share what they "heard" in the narratives.

If the audience does not respond right away, we wait.

We wait until someone in the audience chooses to bridge the space between performer and audience, story and truth.

Sometimes we wait for what can seem forever.

But safe space does not equal comfortable space, for patterns of violence often can become familiar, and silence can be uncomfortable.

So we resist the urge to begin lecturing or telling the audience unhelpful and overused information on safety; rather, we let the safety emerge, reminding ourselves that we do not need to control the audience. That is never our intention.

We have come to trust that the space of thirty seconds or a minute or more of quiet will give birth to a conversation, a dialogue born of the audience's needs, desires, pain, and willingness to share. This conversation continues the dialogical performance that the stories began.

Awkward? Perhaps for a minute or two, but a space then opens up, sometimes in baby steps, toward our shared conversation about violence in a safe, nurturing, and collaborative fashion.

# Character Development

*ELAINE stops writing and speaks directly to the audience.*

ELAINE   Sometime in 2002, we began to talk about creating an activist performance troupe that would perform the narratives I collected from battered women living in a shelter for my book, *Women Escaping Violence*. Since doing the ethnographic field research for that book, working in the shelter, and getting the work published, I had been feeling that the academic production of a book was insufficient in terms of my commitment to working against the abuse and violence many women encounter every day in the supposed safety of their own homes from men who profess to love them. Heather's previous work with HIV education in Texas had led her to a similar performance venue for sharing stories of persons living with AIDS. Our "troubling violence" project seemed like a natural kind of collaborative project.

We worked with the narratives in my book and asked graduate students at the University of Missouri in theatre and folklore studies to join us in our performance efforts. We had several meetings in which we explained our plans and goals (both still quite vague) and just brainstormed with this talented group of people to create our performance project. Several members of the group, including Heather, were seasoned actors and directors. The folklore studies students and I were well versed in the world of ethnography and theories about the role of the ethnographer, but we were novices when it came to performing narratives for an audience. Much of our difficulty stemmed from our concerns about ethnographers taking the onus of "performing" the oral narratives of some of the people in my study. Folklore as a discipline demands field research and has in recent years approached the task of ethnographic work with a

serious eye toward ethics, the positionality of the ethnographer, and
the property rights of individuals, who "own" their narratives, healing
practices, and traditional artistic styles and patterns. Developing
a performance troupe and advocating this venue as appropriate
for field-based narratives from study participants was challenging,
but it helps that many folklorists have embraced stage storytelling,
and some have recently moved toward the creative writing of
ethnography. While, we felt that what we were doing was a bit risky,
we were braced and energized by the encounter.

ELAINE *turns to* HEATHER.

ELAINE  The process is altered from the beginning, but that's what
process is, right?

HEATHER *(nodding in agreement)*  Right. One student in my performance studies class had chosen a narrative from Elaine's book for
her personal experience story performance. This provided a kind of
case study for our ideas. This student was a young woman in her
early twenties, attractive, soft-spoken. She had chosen a story about
a boyfriend who became insanely jealous every time he saw his girlfriend with other people, male or female. This narrative recounts
an incident when he sees his girlfriend in a car with a man from
her workplace; she tells her boyfriend that she is only giving her
coworker a lift home, but the boyfriend becomes irate, loses control,
beats in her car hood with his fists, tries to break her car windows,
rants, and exposes a side of himself that she had never before seen
and found very frightening. The woman eventually marries this man,
but her narrative is reflective: "I should have seen it then," she says, "I
should have known what kind of guy he really was. But I loved him,
and I thought this jealousy was really pretty neat; he cared so much.
But then I learned that wasn't really love; it was something else." This
first performance of a narrative from the book was encouraging. The
audience appreciated the student's performance; her claim to the
story was convincing and powerful.

　　Almost immediately after meeting and discussing which stories from Elaine's book the performers would choose, however, the process began to unfold in ways we had not anticipated. Several of the graduate students came with photocopies of stories they had selected from the book, but others had already found ways to disrupt this neat pattern of selection. The only male in our performance troupe was stymied at first about what his role could be. We had discussed the fact that none of us, including him, wanted his role to be that of an abuser, so we discussed the possibility of him telling one of the stories as though his sister or mother were speaking, but we could tell right away that this wasn't what he wanted to do. When we next met, we were awed by the fact that this man had gone home and written a personal experience narrative about creeping up the basement stairs with his little sister to watch their father throwing plates at their mother, who was crouched in a corner of the kitchen. His narrative was his own. And it spoke about how much he loved his father, revealed his tendency toward anger, and pondered the question of whether he would eventually throw plates at his wife. It was a powerful diversion from our plan that arose at the very onset.

Another member of our new troupe told us after our first session that she had gone home to visit and was telling her family about having to learn a story about domestic abuse for this performance troupe. Immediately, she told us, stories emerged from her family, and she believed that she should not perform one of the narratives from Elaine's book but should instead tell one of their stories. By the next rehearsal, some of this woman's family story had been incorporated into our production.

These first months of our collaboration were emotionally draining for us. The performers came to our meetings prepared to perform stories from Elaine's book as well as their own stories, stories from their families and friends, roommates and sisters. Already our project was becoming more complex than we had imagined.

ELAINE *remembers the challenges she faced in learning how to perform.*

ELAINE  Moving from my role as ethnographer, volunteer at the shelter, professor, writer, and teacher into performer and autoethnographic writer has been an astounding journey for me. My life has been all about field research, teaching, and ethics. Although I have been an academic to the core, I have always believed deeply that human rights and social justice should lie at the heart of anything we do. There are certainly easier things to do than work in a shelter for women escaping violence in their lives. And I was uncomfortable with producing a book about the women's narratives and sitting back, thinking I had done my part. Some people clearly would read my book and would read the women's narratives and gain a better understanding of what it is like to live with violence and to have the strength to leave one's home, material things, jobs, and even sometimes one's children to find a safe place in which to recover and hopefully move on. But few people would do so. I know that. So I am convinced that my collaboration with Heather in performance studies was a critical moment in my life and career. Our early conversations were stimulating, excited, expectant with the promise of what might lie ahead in our work together. We knew that neither we nor our students would receive payment for this hard work; we knew that we were undertaking a project that would only add to our already full schedules and lives. Yet we both knew that this was exactly what we wanted to do. So we began.

As we developed what our performances might look like, my role as the ethnographer seemed important. I needed to be the first performer on the stage, and I needed to give the audience some critical information about the narratives they were about to hear. Audience members needed a context for how I collected some of the stories, a frame in which to receive the narratives. My new life as a performer began rather ominously. At our first rehearsal, five performers sat in a slightly curved row in front of our audience. We all sat in wooden chairs. I stood up and began stiffly:

Welcome. I am Elaine Lawless, and I'm an ethnographer.
Several years ago, I began volunteering in a battered women's

shelter, where I collected the narratives of women living in the shelter to escape from abusive husbands and partners. Although I heard stories all around me in the shelter, none of these stories could be used for the book I wanted to write, because everything in the shelter is confidential and needs to be kept anonymous. So I decided to ask the women if they would tell me their stories on tape. I found an empty room and I began to tape-record all their stories and eventually published most of them in my book, *Women Escaping Violence*.

At this point, I turned on the tape recorder sitting on a chair next to me and said to our first performer, "Tell me your story." And, one after the other, the performers told the stories they had come prepared to tell.

This was a heady moment for me. I could hardly breathe. Here we were, in a darkened, empty playhouse, performing the stories from my book. I was nearly in tears; in fact, several of the stories caused my eyes to fill. I sat there immobilized.

Our discussion following this first rehearsal was fascinating. Again, this was all new to me. Heather, as artistic director, came into her own; she carefully talked with each of us about our performances. She nudged us to work on a wide variety of skills—intonation, pauses (beats), natural gestures, and body movements. She praised us all as she also told us how to enhance our narratives and make the performances far better than they were on this first run.

As for me, she laughed, "You need to not be so *stiff*." And I laughed because I *knew* I was stiff; I was scared to death. I'd never performed before.

**HEATHER** Of course you have. You perform every single day in the classroom. You perform at conferences when you give academic papers on this same material.

**ELAINE** But in those venues, I do not think of myself as a performer. There, I am instead a teacher, an academic, a conference presenter. I know all the performance modes for these contexts. But I have no idea how to perform in our performance troupe.

**HEATHER**  Maybe you could stand and deliver your part to the audience in a more relaxed way—in the way you might teach a class or give a presentation at a conference.

**ELAINE**  That seems more comfortable to me. I can do that with my eyes closed.

# First Run

*ELAINE and HEATHER set up chairs in the middle of the stage and move to the wings, directing people on stage to sit in the chairs as they reenact their first performance.*

**HEATHER**   Our first performance was for the recently organized Campus Task Force against Domestic/Partner Violence.

**ELAINE**   Our campus has a strong domestic violence component in the law school, where Professor Mary Beck teaches third-year law students to work with women who are trying to prosecute their abusers, get orders of protection, get custody of their kids, and get child support.

**HEATHER**   Others on the task force such as Professor Fran Danis teach domestic violence components in their courses. Some work in the dormitories with college men and women. The athletic department is represented on the task force, as are campus religious organizations, the health staff, the counseling staff, and a variety of other groups.

**ELAINE**   A captive audience, really.

**HEATHER**   Everyone was curious and enthusiastic about what we were trying to do, eager to see the production they had been hearing about.

*HEATHER then motions for ELAINE to move center stage and perform her story.*

**ELAINE**   At this first run, I did loosen up—some. I stood before the audience, comfortable, as I might be before a class. I dropped the formal and stiff "Welcome. My name is Elaine Lawless." I introduced myself and talked about my research. I told them about volunteering at the shelter and getting the stories for my book. And I told one story about getting a hotline call that was especially disturbing because the cell phone the woman was using to talk to me went dead, leaving me wondering what had happened to her. I talked probably too long about the research; turned on the tape recorder; asked the person sitting next to me, "Tell me your story"; and sat there with the others in front of our audience as each person told his or her story.

HEATHER   Judging from the responses we got that day and in a variety of e-mails in the days following, our performance was a success.

ELAINE   The audience was enthusiastic about the possibilities this troupe offered to share stories of women living with violence and escaping from it with a wide variety of audiences, from campus groups to community situations.

HEATHER   We were encouraged—

ELAINE   pleased—

HEATHER   even proud of our accomplishments.

ELAINE   Shortly afterward, Heather called me, and we met to talk about the performance.

HEATHER *begins to move the chairs around to fit her new ideas about the performances.*

HEATHER   I have some ideas. Let's change some things, shake it up. Let's have the performers emerge from the audience instead of sitting all together in front and staying there throughout the production. All of us up there detracts from the narrative of the person who is speaking, and everyone was uncomfortable sitting up there through all the performances. We each need to claim the performance space in more mobile ways. We need to stand up, sit down, sit backward on a chair, perhaps. After each performance, the speaker should then move back into the audience.

ELAINE   I get it; we should begin and end in the audience and be one of them. They will recognize each of us as a performer when we go forward.

HEATHER   Elaine, your performance could be—well, more performative. You are still simply doing what you always do—being the teacher, the conference presenter, the academic. Why don't I introduce the troupe, and you perform *your* story?

ELAINE   I think I get it. The audience did not respond to my performance because it was not a performance the way the other stories were performances. So, if you are the facilitator and introduce the troupe, I'll try to learn how to be a performer.

*ELAINE addresses audience.*

When I began the presentation by introducing myself as researcher and academic, I was defeating my role as a performer. I realize I need to perform my own story about gathering the stories. But this is foreign territory for me. How to be the ethnographer talking about my research as a performer? The challenge was immense.

I began to walk daily on the bike trail near my house. I would walk for an hour and think about my performance. I slowly began to realize that to make that shift, I needed to tell my story about working in the shelter. Oddly, this needed to be about *me*, not about the field research, not about the ethnography per se; it needed to be my story about how I gathered the stories of the women living in the shelter. I should try to perform my story. This was another huge challenge for me. I teach ethnographic writing; I know all the scholarship that decries the tendency of ethnographers to turn the ethnographic gaze on themselves to the extent that they become the ethnographic subject. When "objectivity" went out the window, "subjectivity" and all its myriad evil stepchildren—narcissism, egotism, confessional modes of discourse—became the norm. As Frances Mascia-Lees and her feminist colleagues comment in their critical essay on the dangers of postmodern self-reflection, it is sometimes a small step from self-reflexivity to self-immersion and shifting the focus from the ethnographic subjects to a self-absorbed, self-effacing, self-promoting, self-enhancing focus on the ethnographer. I had sought to avoid this position in my work. Conversely, I knew, other theorists claimed that our work is always about ourselves—how could it be otherwise?

When I was writing *Women Escaping Violence*, I wrote a chapter about my personal experiences with domestic abuse, weaving my mother's and grandmother's stories into this chapter. I experimented with creative nonfiction to write a lengthy story about my mother growing up the seventh child in a family of fifteen girls, her mother a midwife but too worn out to do much beyond wipe bottoms and noses and work a hardscrabble farm with my grandfather, who was always angry about the girls my grandmother kept producing—girls who only stayed with farm work so long before leaving for the city or early marriages. My mother met my father at fourteen, married him at fifteen, bore a son just as my father left with a submarine crew for the Philippines during World War II; he came back badly damaged but able to create me, a true baby boom statistic, within weeks of returning home in 1947. I hinted at the abuse and violence I both knew and suspected in my mother's family; I wrote about my own first abusive marriage. Then I took all of this material out of the book; it sits gathering dust underneath my printer at home. I decided this book should not be about me. It needed to be about the women living in the shelter while I was volunteering there; it was their book, their story, not mine. I wrote a narrative about my ethnographic work, but it was an academic rather than a personal enterprise. I was pleased with it. I could not be accused of taking this self-reflexivity too far.

But the performance troupe brought all these issues back to
the front burner. For this performance troupe to work, I needed to
learn how to perform my story for the audiences. I had to shed the
"introduction" mode and create my own personal narrative. I needed
to perform *my story*.

At our next rehearsal session, I tried to tell my story for Heather
and the troupe. I had practiced my story for miles on the trail. I
had not written it out, but I knew what I wanted to include. Later,
I realized that I probably did need to write it out so that I could
visualize on the page the various parts of the story I wanted to tell.
Heather talked with me about the logistics of telling my story—
when one story would fit the best and how to do the business of
using the performance space, the chairs, the tape recorder to the best
advantage before I left the stage and sat again in the audience.

For this rehearsal, I told my story standing before the audience.
I tried not to be standing there the way a "presenter" giving an
introduction might. I tried to think about my body and my words;
I needed to think of myself as a performer performing a story—my
story. It was excruciating. I rushed some parts because I was afraid
the audience (the other members of the troupe and Heather) would
get bored because they had now heard this several times. I obviously
know nothing about rehearsals, where performers have to perform
over and over and over and over again without rushing, going slowly
and carefully so that each take is better than the one before. But the
troupe members knew the drill. They were patient and critical and
understanding and supportive. Here's what I said (more or less):

I've been thinking about how to tell you what it was like for
me to work in the "safe" shelter for battered women. As I think
about it, I believe it was for me the most unsafe place in my life
at the time. Mostly, I was pretty terrified working there. Only a
few streets across town from my academic office, my computers,
my graduate students, and my classes, the shelter was like a
different universe. I did the forty hours of volunteer training

so that I could work in the shelter. And I can clearly remember the first few times I drove to the shelter, parked in the parking lot, and walked up to the huge steel door at the entrance to the unmarked building. I knew to press the buzzer, and I knew to expect the disembodied voice behind the blinds that asked, in a not-very-friendly voice, "Who are you and what do you want?" Well, actually, it wasn't really that gruff, she probably said, "How can I help you?" I could see the blinds separate just an inch; someone in there could see me, but I couldn't see them. "Oh," I said, "I'm Elaine, and I work here." I knew the person at the desk was checking a sheet of new volunteers to make sure I was who I said I was, and then I heard the lock on the huge door release. I knew I had about thirty seconds to open the door before it relatched. It took both hands to pull the door open, not only because it was huge and heavy but also because a vacuum was produced by the fact that the first huge door was followed by a second before I could actually enter the shelter. Actually, it felt more like a prison than a safe place to me. The victims were locked inside, while the bad guys were free on the outside. That seemed really bizarre to me.

Before long, it was me sitting at that desk behind the blinds buzzing people in. As a safe shelter, it was our job to keep the women safe. The location of the shelter is supposed to be a secret, so not just anybody should be able to walk up to the door and get in. I was trained to peek through the blinds and buzz people in.

I remember one afternoon, pretty late in the afternoon, I heard a car pull up in the parking lot and watched through the blinds. A pretty scuzzy guy gets out of this really scuzzy car, looks around, looks right at the building, and then goes to the trunk and opens it. And I'm telling you, I'm sitting there totally believing that this guy is going to pull a sawed-off shotgun out of his trunk and blast the front of the building. At that point, I was hoping that the door and the windows right in front of my face were truly bulletproof. I thought perhaps I might die right

there. I was pretty scared. But I had to chuckle to myself when
the guy pulled out a saw and a toolbox instead of a shotgun.
Apparently, Pat had forgotten to tell me that she had hired this
guy to work on some of the outside windows. But it was always
a bit scary. We were, after all, hiding women from their violent
husbands.

I eventually was trained to answer the hotline as well. You
know when you have a hotline call because a different button
lights up on the phone. That would always give me a moment's
pause. How would I be able to help someone? Would I say all
the right things? So early one Sunday morning, I answered
as I'd been trained, in a calm and helpful voice: "This is the
shelter. How can I help you?" The voice on the other end of the
line was thin, desperate. "How can I keep him from taking my
kids?" Her first words—"How can I keep him from taking my
kids?" I said, "Tell me where you are, and are you safe? Can you
talk to me?" Her reply was quick: "My sister left her husband,
and he took the kids away and she never saw them again.
Tell me how to keep my kids." At this point, I could hear her
children in the background; I knew she was on a cell phone. I
asked her to tell me the town closest to her. She told me, and
I quickly checked the shelter listings and told her that if she
could drive to such and such a town there was a shelter there. I
could give her the number and she could call them and go there
for safety with her kids while she worked this out. "Can you do
that?" I asked. The phone had a lot of static as I heard her say,
"I'm in the car with my kids, but the keys are in the house and
I don't think I can go back in there and get them." I could tell
she was crying, and at that point, the phone went dead. I never
knew what happened to that woman, but I can guess. In fact, I
have an empty chair here today for that woman and for all the
stories I never got to hear [gestures toward an empty chair].

But, of course, I did hear other stories. I heard stories all
the time in the shelter. I heard women tell stories in the kitchen
as we cooked dinners and breakfasts for their kids; I inhaled

secondhand smoke sitting in the smoking room listening to
the women share stories; I heard stories in the office as women
came in for the first time with black plastic bags filled with
clothes, with their kids, and with their broken bones and
bruises; I heard stories shared in the Thursday evening support
group we ran. But I knew I could never use any of those stories
for a book I wanted to write about these women and their
stories of living with violence and escaping it, coming into
shelter, and moving on.

But I decided there was a legitimate way to get their stories.
I began to put signs up all over the shelter—in the kitchen, the
smoking room, the office. My signs said, "Tell me your story.
Elaine, who works in the office, wants to write a book about you
and your experiences with violence. If you are willing to share
your story with her, stop by the office and let her know." Then I
held my breath because I did not know if a single woman would
come to me and offer to share her story. But, you know, they
did. They came, one after the other, for months, willing—eager,
even—to share their stories with me.

I found a mostly empty storage room, and I set up my
tape recorder. This wasn't an interview. I did not ask them any
questions. I just turned on the recorder and said, "Tell me your
story."


I left the "stage" and went into the audience to sit down. I
felt better after giving this performance. And the others, Heather
included, agreed that this was my story and that it worked far better
than the presenter mode I had taken on before. This piece is most
definitely about me. I have shifted my position; I have accepted the
mantle of performer, whatever that means. This *is* my story. This is
the story of how I set out to do something and did it and how it has
affected my life to such a degree that I want to take an activist role in
sharing what I have learned with others who can join me in bringing
a taboo subject into the open, exposing violence in our homes as the

evil it is; bringing men to account for their habits of anger, battering, humiliating, punishing, and isolating their wives and girlfriends; encouraging women and even young girls to leave or find ways to resist fear, abuse, and violence and demand their right to safety, a good life, and peace of mind. We don't need bigger and better shelters—we need to tackle the heart of the problem in our country. Men are allowed to beat and batter women and children. We need concerted efforts at every level—family, community, religious, political, educational, recreational—to eliminate the possibility for one member of a family to hit and emotionally abuse another. This should be recognized as part of our constitutional rights. Why are we guaranteed less within our own homes than we are on our streets? Assault is assault whether or not you know your assailant. Violence is troubling, and we intend to trouble it—over and over again until the picture comes back clear and unmuddied. Safety. Guaranteed.

# Breaking the Fourth Wall*

---

HEATHER *moves into the audience and takes a seat next to an unsuspecting audience member. She begins to talk directly to the woman and simultaneously begins writing in a notebook.*

---

HEATHER   In this part of our book performance, I engage in performative writing to introduce the Troubling Violence Performance Project, a troupe that seeks to open lines of communication about issues of domestic violence through performance of personal narratives. Experimental in nature, this essay seeks to show how story is used to educate audiences about societal issues. Neither the stories of abuse nor the description of our work is polished or neat, and there are certainly no tidy endings.

I have struggled with the ways in which to tell the story of the troupe, for the hundreds of performances in which we have engaged over the past five years have continued to change and redefine the troupe. Performative writing, however, is a way of defying issues of control on the page, just as we seek to defy issues of control in our performance work and our lives. Fred Corey asserts that "no one definition of performative writing can or will exist; the elusive nature of the phrase is a component of its value. If a clear definition existed, if an understanding of the phrase were right or wrong, if a noted scholar authored the final characteristic of the concept, performative writing may well be put to a deserved rest" (Miller and Pelias 2001, xii). Issues of violence are intertwined with how women's voices are presented— and heard—in both the academic and the wider community stage. Just as there is no exact way to identify a potential abuser, there is no exact right—or wrong—way to deal with complex relationships.

*Part of this chapter appears in "This is the story of . . . The Troubling Violence Performance Project," by M. Heather Carver in *Storytelling, Self, Society: An Interdisciplinary Journal of Storytelling Studies*, Volume 4, issue 2, May 2008: 88–101.

Trying to trouble the notions of what contributes to unhealthy relationships and violence toward women, however, is not easy work. So we embrace the difficulty of the writing and engage in performatively weaving in our stories as well as the stories of the troupe.

HEATHER *writes furiously in her notebook.*

~~This is the story of two academics who set out to give voice to the stories of abused women.~~
~~This is the story of a group of citizens who set out to uncover the violence that lurks beneath the rugs of homes across America.~~
~~This is the story of a troupe that wanted to speak truths usually unspoken.~~
This is the story of stopping violence . . .
This is the story of trying to stop violence against women—through story.

*The audience sits and talks a little; some look at their watches, while others check their cell phone messages. Soon there are some announcements, and a couple of women professors are introduced. One thanks the audience for the invitation to share the group's stories and introduces the other one, who wrote a book about domestic violence. She starts talking about working in a shelter, and some of the audience members start to shift uncomfortably. She continues to talk about gathering the stories of violence for her ethnography of the women's shelter. Then she sets a chair aside, says, "This is for the women's stories that we won't hear today," and returns to her seat with the rest of the crowd. There is a bit of a pause, and then a woman sitting in the audience starts to talk as she walks up to the stage.*

KAREN    I can't say that we weren't taken care of well, but my mom worked, OK, full time, and I never understood why she put up with what he did to her. Never. I always—I'd lay at night, and even though I never felt close to my mom, she took very good care of us kids. She

worked a full-time job and he, I guess—he claimed he worked as a
farmer, but now I know, as I grew up and I've talked to her since, you
know, we're still not close, I've learned a lot of things about him.

I hated him from the time I knew, even as a little kid, probably back, I'd say eight or nine, maybe ten at the oldest, what he was
capable of doing. I knew it wasn't right. Because I would go out, even
to school, because we weren't allowed to go anywhere else, OK, we
didn't function like a family. What I would hear and watch on TV,
people saying "I love you," OK, our family wasn't like that. Still to
this day, if I hug my mom or tell my mom that I love her, she's like,
"Why are you doing that?" You know, she can't relate to that, OK,
and I often wonder if it was because she was abused, how she grew
up, or just for the simple fact that he took that away from her. I
believe it's all of it. Her way of taking care of stress in her family is
basically showing, OK, that's the thing. But that abuse went on—he
died when I was fourteen, and I was glad.

But when I met this man, this was like walking into heaven
and—

*Long pause. She is crying.*

he was the most kind and considerate and very loving person I ever
could have begun to imagine. It was me. I got to be involved in this.
*[sobbing]* And we had a good relationship for a long time, but he took
advantage of that relationship. I once again made a mistake in telling
my past, OK? Just things that I guess some people call standards,
OK? Like this time, I thought, I'm not gonna make this mistake
again.

But as we grew closer together, I started to tell him more
and more—he was the only man that knew that my daughter was
born the way she was. He was the only man that knew that I had
problems with alcohol and drugs. He was the only man that knew
about my dad. He was the only man that ever knew I was sexually
molested by my brothers. He knew everything about me. He was
just, like I said, he was what you would call a prince, OK? He was a

fairy tale that was gonna close the doors to the madness that I grew up with. [crying] I was gonna be a hero and live happily ever after with this man. And that never happens, either, so that's why, OK, that's my lost hope, so that's never gonna happen. And I believe it's not. That fairy tale's gone.

He was the first man I ever had been with that you could actually wake up with and [speaking slowly] feel the way I felt when I was with him. He made me feel that way.

And I knew he loved me. I knew there was something there. So we got engaged to be married and this was three—I was starting to see things about him, OK. I'd be like—OK, you know, "You didn't want me to work." Well, he made good money. He was a construction worker. He had his own business. Made like thirty dollars an hour. And I was like, "This can't be happening to me. There is no way. I'm set. This man loves me." He was unreal. I knew that this was where not only that I finally wanted to be with my life, but yet, at times that I deserved—finally, I finally am going to get what I deserve in my life.

He's the type of person that was very materialistic, but he was very giving as well. And I was like—it was just like being in paradise. I never thought this would ever happen to me. But when it ended, it ended like it always does. It's like starting something and being so blown away because you don't want to be spun around on a carousel over and over and over again. Same old shit. It's a repeat. It's a pattern. And I guess I have it. We all have it. What is it? We like abuse; I've been told that. You like it; that's why you stay in it. See, normal people would think, "Just think about the abuse." I try to do that. I try so hard. "Go back to the night when he cracked your ribs. Go back to the night when he took your head and hit it with his head so hard it busted your nose open and left you with two black eyes. To where you couldn't even walk for three months. You were in a bed. Go back to that." And like, I can but it, it's like OK. Yeah, he did all that, and I stayed with him then. It's like I think I could change it. But then I wonder, "Well, why haven't you made that call? What are you so afraid of? Are you afraid of rejection?"

*The performer stops talking, nervously looks around, and without any fanfare returns to her seat.*

HEATHER    My heart is pounding as I recall the performances and the narratives of the troupe. Moments from the troupe encircle my mind. Moments that quickly appear, then flash out of sight again. Thump.

An audience member begins to talk about how women just need to "run away." She begins describing a situation that sounds like stranger attack and rape. "Escape!" she repeats. I nod and listen and then respond to the horrors of violent attacks on women in their own homes. It's not that simple, I say. I carefully weave in a few words about how escape is so much more complex and difficult for women who *know* (and even love) their attackers. I try *not* to compare different types of violence toward women with judgment—it is just as ludicrous to say stranger rape is better or worse than intimate partner violence as it would be to say that breast cancer is better or worse than ovarian cancer. It is just different. And what is different about intimate partner violence is that just telling a woman to run away is more than simplistic, it is irresponsible. Women who cannot get away because of their children or because of lack of money or because they have nowhere to go or because they fear violence against their family members are left feeling even more guilt, shame, and isolation.

Thump. Thump.

The professor of the class for which we have just performed asks the students, "So, when were you 'engaged' during this performance, and where did you go when you were not 'engaged'?"

(This was an odd question we had not ever heard asked before, but its appropriateness became very apparent as the students began to respond.)

One student raised her hand and said that she missed some of one of the narratives because she was so suddenly struck by the relevance of the stories to her own life. She had begun making a mental list of her own relationships and those of her friends—thinking about how issues of power, control, and aggression appeared in all of them. She was most present with the nature of our performative work, she said, during her mental absence. Her comments made us wonder how many of our audience members had similar experiences during our performances as the stories sparked listeners' memories and brought a kind of personal confrontation in their minds as our stories filled the room. Or how many of these thought processes continued long after the narratives had been told and we had all started back to our own homes.

When Elaine and I began this project to "trouble violence," we intended to use narratives from her previously published book of women's narratives collected in women's shelters. But after each performance, we came to expect that one or more audience members would approach us, hoping to share his or her story with us and promising to give us that story on tape for our use in future performances.

Thump.

Thump.

As the troupe matured, our student performers also began to tell their own narratives of intimate violence or narratives that had been given to them by family members or friends. Our work became a direct outlet for the narratives of our performers and our collective audiences.

Overwhelming, challenging, difficult, and uncomfortable, yet intensely powerful.

Thump.

Breathe.

Thump.

Breathe.

*Another woman from the back slowly walks to the front of the room and stands behind a chair, leaning on it and then sighing as she slouches down. She seems reluctant as she begins to speak, and she smiles out of nervousness.*

**TAYNA**   I was "that girl" in high school. You know the one, the one that never does anything wrong. I got good grades, went to church every Sunday, youth group every Wednesday; I was a cheerleader, and I never drank or smoked and very rarely swore. I am not that girl anymore, but I'm not a bad girl either. I'm something in between. But then I was, and I wanted to do everything right. So when Adam asked me out, I wanted to date him, because he was "that guy." He was good-looking. He was a year older than me, played sports, and he was really funny. My father said that I couldn't date him. He didn't give a reason really; he didn't really have one. But Dad said he didn't trust him.

I didn't know what to do. I really wanted to be the good girl, but I really liked this guy. So, as any sixteen-year-old, I pushed my limits and I defied my father, and I started sneaking around with Adam. And at first, things were really fun. We had secret rendezvous, and we would laugh and talk. It was like that for about five months, and then he started to pressure me to have sex with him. And even though I was breaking my parents' rules, I wasn't ready to throw the baby out with the bathwater and become a "bad girl." So I wouldn't have sex with him, and he started to get very angry with me. And then on Valentine's Day, he got really mad when I wouldn't fool around. We were in his car, and he started yelling at me and calling me awful names. So I started yelling back, and then he got really pissed. He shoved my face against the window; he stuck his elbow in my throat and twisted my arm behind my back while threatening to tell my dad that we had been sneaking around. And all I could think was, "If he breaks my arm, how am I going to explain this?"

Anyway, I got him to let go of me by scratching my arm. I was bleeding, and he was kind of a freak about his car. So he let go of me because he didn't want bloodstains in his car. After that night, I wasn't dating Adam any longer. But he didn't leave me alone. I tried to avoid him, and I tried to make sure I was never by myself. But it was really hard, because no one knew that we had been dating, and I didn't want anyone to know what had happened because I didn't want to disappoint my parents. I was kind of stuck, and he knew I was. And of course, one night in May he caught me alone.

Adam lived next door to my best friend, Lindsey. And one night, we were going to have a girls' night. We were going to go out to dinner and then catch a movie, but I was late—practice ran late. And when I got to Lindsey's, she had left, but Adam was waiting for me. He was drunk, really drunk. He told me that Lindsey went to pick up the rest of my friends and she would be back in half an hour, and then she would come and get me from his house. I didn't trust him, nor should I. But he promised not to hurt me and said that we would watch TV and he wouldn't bother me. And that's what happened—for the first fifteen minutes. He got out a water gun and started to shoot me with it, and I was getting really wet, so I took the last sip of water that I had in a glass and threw it him and ran for the door. But it was locked, and as I was trying to unlock it, he grabbed me by the hair and dragged me into the bathroom and threw me against the towel rack, chest first. I hit the wall so hard I lost my breath. He turned on the faucet in the bathtub and stuck my head underneath it, and then the tub started to fill with water and I couldn't breathe, and I thought he was going to kill me. And so I kicked him, I don't know where, but whatever I did he let go and crumpled to the floor. And I ran, as I unlocked the door, Lindsey was standing there with all of my friends. They asked me what happened. I said, "Nothing, I'm fine, Adam is just really drunk." And we left. No one said anything else about it.

And then Adam graduated, and I had another year of high school left. I was starting to feel better about things because he had taken a summer job on the East Coast and I hadn't seen him all summer. But he came back to town for a couple of weeks just before he started college. I didn't know he was back, so I wasn't being careful. And he caught me alone one night. He told me to get into his car, and I said no. I said he was crazy and mean and I didn't want to talk to him ever again. And he said that he was on his way to a party with all of our friends, he wanted to give me a ride, and he said that he would be nice and gentlemanly. And I told him that I had heard it all from him before and I didn't believe him. And then he said he would tell my dad, and I don't know why, but that really got to me. So I got in the car. It was perhaps the stupidest thing I have done in my life.

Well, he didn't take me to the party. He took me somewhere else. And, he—well, he forced me to have sex with him.

*She chuckles nervously and uncomfortably.*

I guess some people call that rape. I got really depressed after that happened. I quit cheerleading, I stopped dressing cute, and I gained some weight—not a lot, but some. I didn't go out anymore; I stayed at home and just studied. Books seemed safer than people. I didn't tell anyone about that night for a long time. It was almost two years before I could talk about it. I didn't tell anyone until I came to college.

I didn't see him after that night for a long time. He went to school, and whenever he came into town, I made sure that I was safe in my house. And then I started college, and I started to feel better again. I got away from all of that stuff. I got good grades, made new friends, started going out, and began to dress cute again. I guess I started drinking a lot—too much. But I've cut back on the drinking this semester. It didn't seem like a good habit to get into.

I don't know. Last year, my freshman year, went well; he left me alone. But he started calling in September. I always hang up, but that doesn't stop him from calling. And now he's started to come to the store I work at. He buys a pack of twenty-five-cent gum and just stares at me. It isn't a mean stare, but it makes me uncomfortable. I don't know what he wants or what he is going to try to do, but I really wish he would leave me alone.

TAYNA *frowns, pulls herself up, and returns to her seat in the audience.*

**HEATHER**    Whoa. Another performance races into my mind. Slow down and breathe.

This performance had begun long before our arrival and has no ending in the near future.

Then where to begin telling this story?

Perhaps it was how off-guard I was—we were—with the audience of the event.

Perhaps it was the 250-plus mostly male athletic coaches staring at us as we took the stage.

Perhaps it was seeing a coach in the crowd who had thrown a chair into a ten-thousand-dollar plasma television screen a couple of weeks earlier to "motivate" his team.

Perhaps it was the glare of the athletic director, who sat in the front row—patronizing, smug, distant.

Perhaps it was the two women who came to us with their stories afterward.

Perhaps it was my student performer who took the brunt of the ugly responses from the coaches.

Perhaps it was more.

But I know that something made the athletic department ask us not to return.

Something indeed.

*A young man emerges from the audience and starts to approach the front of the room. Several audience members frown, shift in their seats, and there is a tension that spreads until he begins speaking and they realize he is telling the story not of an abuser but of a child watching his mother fend off plates thrown by his angry father.*

**STEPHEN**    I don't remember much from when I was young. But along with the memory of my uncle pushing me off a steep hill in my big wheel in a drunken stupor and my other uncle, also in a drunken stupor, pulling me a quarter of a mile on an inner tube while I was completely submerged underwater, I remember the thrown plates.

Why it sticks out so clearly, I don't know. My father has done many worse things. But the plates were a powerful image. I was probably six or seven. It was evening but before dinner. I was in the basement cross-training on a Nintendo game. Nowadays you can put a game in and rest assured that sooner or later you will beat it. But back then, it was like an Olympic sport. You had to train for months to even have a shot. My sister was behind me on the sofa, listening to "Little Red Corvette" on the stereo my dad got when he first started teaching eighth-graders. Somewhere in the mix with the harpsichord-like melody of the game, Rygar, and Prince moaning "Baby, you're much too fast," I heard shouting from upstairs. At this point in my life, this only sent off minor alarms in my mind. Shouting was nothing new. It was certainly no cause to shut off the game or the record. Suddenly, though, a new sound entered the picture, the sound of something breaking. That got our attention. I paused the game and turned down the TV. My sister made Prince's shriek into a whisper. We snuck up the basement stairs and opened the door to the kitchen a small crack.

My dad does this thing when he's pissed off. In Tolkien's books, Gandalf does a magic trick that makes his voice boom and his character fearsome. What my dad does is similar. When he is in a good mood, he seems like a normal enough guy. But when he gets angry, he puffs up like a blowfish and his voice sounds like the devil. The image my sister and I saw through the crack was of this strange character, still our father, but something else altogether. My mom was in the corner, by the fridge, crying on the floor. My dad was throwing our dinner plates all around her. Now, he wasn't throwing them *at* her. That's not at all what my dad was about back then or what he's about now. Everything is intimidation with the man. For some bizarre reason, making that clear makes me feel better. When my sister and I saw what was going on, we closed the door and started crying together. After a while, we got up and opened the door and I guess we thought we were going to try to calm things down. My mom shot up and ushered us up to our rooms. We didn't even try to fight it. We went up to my sister's room and cried some more, waiting for the storm to break. Eventually it did. My dad left. And sometime later that night we had macaroni and cheese on paper plates.

I don't know anything about abuse. I know that I have never once entertained the idea that I lived in an abusive household, even though things like this were a regular occurrence. I just assume that events like this go on in every house in America and it gets swept under the rug. No big deal. I don't know what abuse is like for women. I don't pretend to. I'm not haunted. I don't have nightmares. I don't even think about it that much. Despite it all, I don't even have negative associations with my dad. In fact, there's only one thing I worry about. Maybe this is a guy thing, or maybe it plagues everybody that has ever lived around abuse. I do worry that someday it'll be me throwing the plates. I mean, I get mad. I have a bad temper. I've never hurt a fly, but I did punch a hole in a door once. So I worry that someday, it'll be me.

And you know what makes it worse? Several of my ex-girlfriends have told me that when I'm angry, I'm not at all like myself. One even told me that when I get really pissed off, I sound totally different—kind of like the devil.

*When* STEPHEN *is finished, he hangs his head as he passes another woman who has risen from her chair. She is confident, strident, even angry. She uses strong language to tell about the "son of a bitch" who tried to kill her, and the audience seems to hang on her every word. Does she escape?*

*After a couple more stories, the first professor, with the short hair returns. She introduces the storytellers as they put chairs into a semicircle in front of the audience. She is loud and confident as she asks the audience a question.*

PROFESSOR    So what did you hear?

*No one speaks.*

*She waits. The other storytellers look at her, the floor, the audience.*
*No one speaks.*

*She continues to wait. The other professor waits. The group sits*
*calmly.*

**AUDIENCE MEMBER 1**    Thank you.

*The professor smiles warmly.*

**AUDIENCE MEMBER 2**    I heard a lot of pain in those stories.

*Another audience member in the back agrees and then adds her percep-*
*tion of the trauma of the women in the stories. And the conversation*
*begins.*

**HEATHER**    We soon went beyond creating a safe space for discussion of the problem to providing a space where women could con-
template their own stories as they related to those performed by the
troupe members. The encounter had enabled them to step forward
and say that they were now ready to tell their own stories and give
them to the troupe for future performances. The work's social activist goals were growing exponentially: women's stories of battering
and abuse were being told publicly; discussions of this taboo topic
resulted directly from the telling of these women's stories; the telling
of the stories and the discussions were leading women in the audience as well as the performers to acknowledge their private situations, claim their stories. They were becoming empowered to come
forward to say they had encountered violence and abuse.

Over the past five years, we have continued to tell stories. It is
not easy, and it is not always smooth. But after *every* performance
we have given, someone has come up to one of us in the troupe
and offered to give us their story of abuse on tape for the troupe to
perform. Sometimes shaking, sometimes bright red with embarrass-
ment, sometimes calm, they come forward, just as they came forward

in the women's shelter to share their stories with Elaine in her initial
ethnographic work.

. . .

More memories of the troupe over the past years cut deep into my
thoughts—hard. I remember our first performance to the women's
activist group on campus, and then I see the faces of the women from
the time we performed for some shelter residents.
    Staring.
    Quiet.
    Ashamed.
    There.
    When I think about the performances that stand out in my
mind, I realize that it wasn't the narratives we told—although they
are important—but the relationship that we established in the
moment with each different audience discussion. We made a commitment to be present with the audience—and we were. And we
will be again the next time we perform. There is no room for canned
responses in this work. We have to think on our feet, and we have to
embody our thoughts.
    You see, there's a lot about the troupe that doesn't mark the
pages—the hidden truths of our members, for example. Each of us
has a personal past filled with or without violence, immediate or just
next door.

. . .

Piling into my minivan, we laughed and hauled ourselves out of our
Columbia lives and journeyed to St. Louis. This was not an eagerly
anticipated trip. We were four—two graduate students plus Elaine
and me—and a member who had graduated and had moved to St.
Louis was to join us there to perform. It didn't seem enough as we
arrived at the slick new theater on the campus of the University of
Missouri at St. Louis. We seemed somehow too small for the enor-
mity of the task, the space. So I decided that I would also perform. I
shared my story about my school friend whose sports celebrity father

shot her mother and then himself. I didn't tell their story as much as
my own—my encounters with violence while growing up—not in
my own home, but all around me. I told about my father's colleague
who killed his wife and buried her at the lake. I shared my frustration
with the fact that all women have either been violated or have almost
been—it is too rare for a woman not to have had unwanted sexual or
violent attentions—overwhelming to imagine. Frustrating. Perplexing.

This was not one of my finer performative moments—I had
been better and certainly would do more creative performance work
in the years to come. But I remember the faces of the women in the
audience. And I remember the expression on my former student's
face when he talked about his abusive father.

The chairs were red.

My heart was heavy.

But if I thought I was tired, what about that woman in the tenth
row who never said a word but whose eyes told a story with which
we were ever so familiar?

. . .

*Reader*: OK, but what is the Troubling Violence Performance Project
*doing* through telling stories?

*Short Answer*: We are:

- Troubling notions of gender—women in the academy,
  women in the home, women in the field, women as
  scholars/artists.
- Troubling violence—violence originates in the early notions
  of gender roles.

*Longer Answer*: As long as we diminish the power and status of
women in our culture, there will be violence. Through the unfolding tales of women who experience violence in the home, we seek to
explore the culture of uneven gender roles that leads to the culture
of violence. We speak, we talk, we discuss. The Troubling Violence
Performance Project does not have all of the answers or an easy

solution to the problem, but we know that if we aren't part of the conversation, if we don't begin the conversation, if we don't contribute to the communication about abusive behavior, then it is as if we are condoning violence toward women. This is the story of the Troubling Violence Performance Project, a performance troupe that seeks to educate audiences on the university campus and throughout the wider community about intimate partner violence.

And our stories begin to give voice to the call, "not again, no more, no longer!"

*HEATHER moves back onto stage and joins ELAINE at the table.*

**ELAINE**   So, how do we put this thing together?

**HEATHER**   It's beginning to feel too linear to me.

**ELAINE**   It doesn't fall out in a particular pattern of "this is the most important" or "this is less important," so how do we lay this out?

**HEATHER**   I'm always saying to people, Perform the story. There's really no beginning, middle, or end. There's really no model for how to tell this story as it happened during the last three years.

**ELAINE**   This is making me really nervous. But I'm trying to get into your head, because when I do, then I understand what you mean by *performative writing*.

**HEATHER**   Well, I'm not just talking about performative writing. I'm also talking about control and the way in which in our performances with the troupe we really seek to provide a comfortable space for the audience to respond to our work in a noncontrolling environment, so on purpose we don't have an agenda that's stated, we don't have PowerPoint, we don't have handouts, we don't say, "This is what an abuser look like." Rather, we create a space, even a small space, with whomever is there. We create a space for dialogue about this taboo subject. We're professors who are of course capable of setting out a complete set of guidelines, but we resist. It's important to resist having a list of topics and an agenda.

# Performing Violence

*ELAINE leans back in her chair, contemplative and engaged.*

**ELAINE** All right. What you're saying reminds me of our first public performance at my national conference. No longer were we on our own campus, talking to women on the Violence against Women Committee; we went public there to my colleagues, some of whom, I knew, might be opposed to what we were doing. Do you remember how Sadie responded to that performance?

**HEATHER** Yes—I remember how flustered she was to do that performance at a conference, so much different from her previous dramatic work, performing these real women's narratives for an academic audience quite new to her. She sent an essay about her experience at the conference to me by e-mail, and it eventually even became a chapter in her dissertation.

*As the two women continue to recall their experiences, SADIE, a former graduate student and founding member of the troupe, emerges to tell her story to the audience as a monologue.*

**SADIE** After I finally committed to the troupe, I felt like I was in a special period. Much like Stephen said, "We're the new Wooster Group." I was impressed with the positive effect that the troupe had on most audiences. After our first performance, we suddenly found our troupe being booked very quickly. Every time I opened my e-mail, there was a new message from Elaine or Heather asking for volunteers for a new performance.

I was also impressed with Elaine and Heather's research in the area of studying and performing narratives. Most of the research presented in my graduate classes made an academic call for the type of work we were doing. For example, in *Strategies of Qualitative Inquiry*, Norman Denzin and Yvonna Lincoln discuss the impact that the crisis of representation has had on qualitative research. From the mid-1980s forward, scholars have had to be aware of the reflexive turn, which calls into question the relationship of the researcher with the research. Questions of who represents whom, what is represented, and the manner in which culture is represented began to emerge. Of course, the crisis has not been resolved in twenty-plus years. Scholars scream across academic boundaries, "My way is better than yours!" And scholars often argue within disciplines about the best methodological practices. I had read about the ethical debates, and I was intrigued about how we would be received by folklorists and ethnographers when we performed for them.

As we flew into Albuquerque for the American Folklore Society meeting on October 10, 2003, Stephen leaned to look out the window at the night sky. The moon was full and rising over the plateaus that surrounded the city.

"This is the bee's knees," he said.

I smiled and nodded in agreement.

We arrived at the hotel and saw Janet and Charla standing outside waiting for us. We all started chatting immediately, talking about our flights, taxi drivers, and of course what we thought was going to happen the next day after the performance.

As an outsider from theater, I found myself oblivious to cultural politics embedded in the discipline of folklore.

Janet said, "I don't know how this is going to go."

Charla nodded her head in agreement.

"What do you mean?" I asked.

"Well, Elaine is probably going to ruffle some feathers with this one," Stephen said.

"How?" I asked.

Charla said, "This isn't traditional ethnography."

"And some of her fans aren't going to like it," Stephen said.

I did not understand; I thought our work was traditional. Cultural anthropologists, ethnographers, folklorists, and performance studies scholars had worked together before, creating similar projects from collaborative research. I did not understand what was nontraditional about the troupe. No one got naked. No one defecated on anything. And there certainly was no smearing chocolate on vaginas.

"Wait a second," I said. "What do you mean, Elaine has fans?"

"Elaine is important in the field," Janet said.

"I know she edits the *Journal of American Folklore*," I said, proving what little knowledge I had.

"She does more than edit a journal," Charla said.

"You'll see," Stephen said.

I felt like an idiot and desperately wanted to go home. I had been in Albuquerque for an hour, and this trip was already more than I imagined and wanted. I had gone to the conference for two reasons. First, I desperately needed to put a line on my vita; more importantly, I wanted to help Elaine. Nowhere in my personal itinerary was the line, "You are going to have your research ethics scrutinized."

In my hotel room, on the afternoon of the performance, I stood in front of a mirror and looked at my clothing choices. I didn't know what to wear. I had brought two outfits to the conference; one included a blazer and glasses. The other was an all-black ensemble with a burgundy scarf for color. I had chosen the black outfit, the universal costume of an actor. But I as I stood pondering my reflection, I second-guessed myself. Perhaps I looked too much like an artist, and my dress might undermine the troupe's merit in the eyes of a skeptical audience. I didn't know if I was supposed to be an artist or a scholar. From what Janet, Stephen, and Charla had said, I couldn't be both at the American Folklore Society.

In a panic, I started rubbing off my eyeliner and checked the clock. After I had successfully smeared charcoal-colored goo all over my face, I didn't have time to change. I grabbed a light sweater in case it was cool in the conference room and ran for the door.

Outside of the conference room, I saw Stephen.

"Chandler, you look like an actress," he said.

"I know, I know. I struggled with what to wear." I turned to Janet. "Do I look OK? Is it too much?"

Janet hesitated. I knew that I had made the wrong choice; I should have worn the blazer.

"You look fine," she said.

God love her, she was trying to make me feel comfortable in the strange world I had walked into. I went into the room where we supposed to perform and my face went white.

Janet looked at me, "Are you OK? You look sick."

"Why is the room so big? Why are there so many chairs?" I asked.

I could feel my stomach churning. Regardless of what I had been told about Elaine's reputation, I was not prepared for a large audience. I thought if you were a famous academic you might get twenty-five people in the room. I did not count chairs, but I swear there were at least two hundred chairs in the room. I had a sudden urge to throw up.

"I gotta go," I said as I ran to a bathroom.

As I left the room, I heard Janet ask, "Is she going to be able to perform?"

"Yeah," said Stephen. "She always pukes before a performance. She'll be fine."

When I came back to the conference room, all of the troupe members were gone except for Elaine.

"Where did everyone go?" I asked.

"Outside," she said.

I hurried out to look for my peers. I found Janet and Stephen standing under the awning of the hotel, taking a few breaths of fresh air before we performed.

"I would stay out here with you, but I need to go to the restroom before we start. Are you going to be OK?" Janet asked.

"Yeah," I said.

"I'll stay out here with her," Stephen said.

He did not last long. I was pacing and mumbling to myself. Finally he said, "You're so nervous, you're making me nervous. I have to go to the bathroom. Oh, and you need to make sure the door stays propped; otherwise you'll be locked out." He left.

Of course, during one of my pacing stretches, someone walked by and removed the door prop. I looked at my watch; I only had a few minutes to run around the hotel, enter the front, and go down a flight of stairs to the conference room. To top it all off, it had been drizzling when I went outside, but as soon as I heard the door lock, a downpour started. Why, why, why was this happening? None of it helped my nerves.

I ran around the building, down the stairs, and into the conference room. I pulled my wool sweater over my head as I ran outside. I did not want to look like a drowned rat if my research ethics were going to be scrutinized.

Fortunately, the black outfit I had on didn't show water spots, but the sweater was drenched. I caught a glimpse of myself in the mirror. I looked terrible. But I didn't have time to worry about it; it was showtime. I took my designated seat in the audience, slipped into character, and waited to share my story.

I tried to put myself in the correct frame of mind when the troupe gathered in front of the room for the postperformance discussion. I went over a mantra that I made up on the spot.

*I perform with the troupe to stimulate dialog.*

*I am at the conference to speak to the silence that surrounds abuse.*

*I am here to better the lives of women.*

Janet, Stephen, and Charla were right; we ruffled some feathers—or, more accurately, Elaine ruffled feathers. It seemed like the audience interrogated Elaine. Again, I felt like I was in the middle of a foreign country, but this time there were bullets whizzing by. From our aesthetics to our ethics, all of our choices were dissected.

"Why did you choose to stage the piece as if we were in church and you are giving testimony?"

I thought to myself, "It's called metatheater. And we come from the audience to imply that violence can happen to anyone, even the person sitting next to you."

Elaine explained the rationale behind Heather's artistic decision to put the performers in the audience.

"What about how you are representing the Other? So much can be changed through performance."

I thought, "Yes, bodies and voices affect the interpretation of the stories, but our performing is no different than the writing of a narrative. Interpretative choices are made when you put a period or comma on the page. But more importantly, we are doing something special here: we are trying to use research to effect social change."

Elaine responded by saying that she shared the audience members' concerns, but she wanted her research to reach a wider audience. Performance offered the opportunity to reach women who might be in need but could not obtain a copy of her book or women who were currently living in crisis.

Elaine's polite answer reminded me of Denzin and Lincoln's search for a remedy to the crisis of representation: "Epistemologies from previously silenced groups emerged to offer solutions. . . . The concept of the aloof observer has been abandoned. More action, participatory, and activist-oriented research is on the horizon" (1994, 54). There we were on the horizon, and we were meeting severe academic resistance. Surely these audience members had read Denzin and Lincoln; perhaps the audience had an issue with them as well. I really wished *they* were in the audience.

"And what about the performers—how do you feel about the ethics of performing this kind of work?"

I thought, "The ethics that I am primarily concerned with are subverting the sexist, racist, homophobic, classist culture we live in. This work does that; furthermore, our ethics have been impeccable in the formation of this troupe."

"I grew up in a violent home," a woman said through tears.

While this audience member's response was more in tune with our goals, I suddenly got very uncomfortable. At MU, we performed with a therapist present. At that point in the discussion, my mind left the conversation. The emotional highs in the room were too much for me.

I studied the audience. It was comprised of mostly women. The majority of the men in the audience seemed to be Elaine's graduate students and one colleague from MU. I thought it was completely reprehensible that men were absent. My brain sounded off, "Violence is not a women's issue. Men do this to us."

But I didn't say a word; I sat silently in the face of academic abuse.

After the interrogation was over, Stephen, Janet, Charla, and I gathered to assess the situation.

"That wasn't that bad," Stephen said.

"What? That was terrible," I said.

"No, it could have been worse," Janet said.

"Yeah, I was expecting a lot worse," Charla said.

"It gets worse?" I asked.

"Oh, yeah. You should see some of the comments we get at the journal for articles that are a lot less controversial than what we're doing," Janet said.

"Academics are mean," I said.

"I noticed you were uncharacteristically quiet," Stephen said to me.

"I didn't know what to say," I said.

Actually, the audience backlash had slapped the words and thoughts out of my mouth. It would take me a long time to make meaning of the events that transpired in that conference room. The scholarship of Denzin and Conquergood helped me to make sense of the folklore conference.

In 2003, Denzin called for performance: "The current historical moment requires morally informed performance and arts-based disciplines that will help people recover meaning in the face of senseless, brutal violence, violence that produces voiceless screams of terror and insanity" (7). After I read Denzin's statement, I threw my arms up in triumph and committed to taking up the banner by using performance in conjunction with sociological research to perform the silenced voices. However, from Boston to Portland, each time the troupe performed for an academic conference, some person would be uncomfortable with the manner in which we were presenting the research participants. The resistance from ethnographers dumbfounded me. Denzin was not alone in his call for performance of ethnographic research. Conquergood's research with Hmong refugees brought about the idea of dialogical performances as a way to conduct meaningful ethnographic research (2003). When leaders in the field such as Denzin and Conquergood were making a case for performance ethnography, I did not understand where the academic backlash was coming from.

I later considered the crisis of representation a little more deeply. According to Denzin and Lincoln, ethnographers are in a triple crisis, where "the ethnographer's authority remains under assault" (2003, 28). They go on to explain there have been several moments during which ethnographers' validity and reliability have been questioned to create a more ethically sound methodology. I thought about those ethnographers on a personal level. I assumed each scholar had personally struggled with this crisis and had to come to realizations of the Self in relation to his or her work. I imagined such struggles were at times painful and hard-won. Therefore, when we came marching in performing research, we called into question each scholar's personal struggle with his or her work. Of course there was resistance!

However, Elaine's sound original research and Heather's direction had put us in a strong position. Heather's artistic contributions adhere to Conquergood's dialogical performance, which "struggles to bring together different voices, world views, value systems, and beliefs so that they can have conversations together," seeking "to bring self and other together so that they can question, debate, and challenge one another" (1985, 5). So we were presenting ethnographic work that responded to Ruth Behar (1996, 8): "Call it sentimental, call it Victorian and nineteenth century, but I say that anthropology that doesn't break your heart just isn't worth doing anymore."

While I cannot deny the fact that my body and my voice affect the original authors' voices, I fervently believe that we who perform with the Troubling Violence Performance Project seek to honor the women who trusted us with their stories. Furthermore, my interpretations of these narratives are no different than those of ethnographers who choose to use the printed word. Regardless of our medium, we make choices that affect the presentation of the research—printed punctuation or voice inflection. The important issue is to end this violence against women and the social injustice that many women have experienced and continue to endure. In Elaine's words, we are "In speaking loudly the abuse, the violence, the damage done to our minds and bodies, our united voices must reach a crescendo that will translate, eventually, into political clout and a stance of *no tolerance* for abuse ever, to another woman by a man" (Lawless 2001, 158). This is more than an ethical research methodology. It is a noble and moral act.

ELAINE, HEATHER, *and the audience applaud* SADIE *as she exits the stage with a triumphant flair.* HEATHER *and* ELAINE *smile as they sit again at the umbrella table near the water, writing in their notebooks. They occasionally stop to share thoughts.*

HEATHER   We have been talking so much about the troupe today. Sometimes it is hard for me to keep up with my racing thoughts that scatter like the gravel along the road with each step we take as we walk the lake path.

ELAINE   And the stories mingle with the reality of our lives and those of our students, our friends. Four days ago, Jackie, a middle-aged African American female student, sat in my office trying to talk with me about her seminar paper. All semester she had pushed us in the class to approach our reading of novels in terms of the gender of the characters and how the writer did or did not address the issue of male empowerment. I had to wonder if the rest of the class got a little tired of hearing her yet again frame her classroom remarks about how Sethe in Toni Morrison's novel, *Beloved*, had been empowered even as she heard Schoolteacher's arrival at her gate and slashed the throat of her girl child. Jackie clung to this interpretation for every text we read in that class. Now she sat in my office explaining how she would write her paper on Linda Hogan's novel, *Power*, in terms of the empowerment of the young native girl who followed in the footsteps of Ama, a wise, old native woman whom the girl saw not only as a kind of mother figure but also a powerful shaman of the tribe.

Jackie had made connections with her reading of the novel with my book, *Women Escaping Violence*, which I had loaned to her. The book had had a tremendous impact on her, she told me. She had read it through one afternoon, and she knew it could help her write her paper on this lost native girl. She then told me she wished we had read my book in our class and resisted my view that the book did not fit the course topic of "folklore and literature." It *was relevant*, she insisted, to everything we had read in the class, especially the critical topic of women's empowerment.

Suddenly, the air in my office changed. The space between this woman and me became palpable with pain and suffering. I could hear her cries in the still air of that third-floor office, high in the trees of the campus, even as the clock ticked and she made not a sound. And with each sharp intake of breath, I *knew*. I *knew* this woman had been talking about herself all semester as she had insisted we consider how women might possibly gain empowerment. Big tears rolled down her perfectly shaped cheek, leaving trails on her luminous skin.

Embarrassed, she carefully kept wiping the tears that would not stop flowing, first from one cheek, then from the other, unable to stop the flow once it began. I held my breath.

"I don't know why I'm crying like this," she said quietly, continuing to catch the tears as they left her wide eyes. "How embarrassing to sit here in my *professor's* office and cry like a baby. I just don't know why I'm crying. I'm so sorry."

"You do not need to be sorry," I replied as gently as I could. But

I checked myself. I did not probe. I did not ask even one question, though her story was so close to the surface I could almost read it on her body. I knew what she would say if I asked her anything. But I also knew not to ask. Not then, not there. She needed to write a paper; she needed to finish the semester; she needed *not* to crumble in her professor's office.

Smoothly, then, without looking her in the eye, trying to ignore the hidden terror and confusion there, I moved us into a safe place where we could talk about the girl in the novel and Jackie's upcoming paper deadline.

Yesterday, I turned in my grades. In a week or so, I will contact Jackie and ask her if she would like to meet. And then I'll wait and see if it feels right to ask her. If it does, I will ask her if she would like to talk. I wonder if she would like to tell me her story.

**HEATHER** Bonnie began her personal narrative performance in my class on autobiography by saying that her life had been framed by males. She didn't name names or even say "my dad" or "my uncle," but rather she separated a chair, a rug, and some stacked beer cans for different "worlds" in which she interacted with each male relationship.

I don't remember the exact details, but I do remember that when she got to the beer cans, she knocked them over and immediately crouched behind the table, cowering and saying "No." That was terrifying. My heart started pounding very fast, and big circles of sweat formed beneath my armpits. She moved on to the next relationship, and I remember something about a sweatshirt giving her comfort after a beloved man passed away. I remember the fear in her voice and the turn of her head as she held up her arm to ward off a blow. When the performance was over, we clapped. There were only a handful in the class.

I cried.

This is something I do not do often—cry in class. While there may be crying in drama, there is usually no crying in academia—well, in front of others, anyway, especially a class.

But I cried.

I cried for my student who had lived in those relationships and for all the other women who still do. I know crying doesn't help anyone. Telling her it was a great performance felt so superficial. But that's what she wanted—to please her professor. And I, who rally against oppression and violence, could not make peace with the idea that I was awarding her a grade for this private moment. What could I say?

Bravo?

Thank goodness you are here?

Well done?

I gave her an A, but we did not talk about the relationship with the abuser. I gave her books about abusers and told her about our performance troupe. But I haven't pried. I don't know if I will. I'm not sure I know what I can handle anymore, so I did call a therapist, and with Bonnie's permission, made her an appointment.

Is that enough?

Is anything?

What *do* I ask for when I ask my students to perform their *lives*?

ELAINE Matthew worked in outreach for the athletic department. He had contacted us about bringing the troupe over to the athletic facility to perform for a group of coaches. His job was to bring appropriate programming to the athletic department.

In truth, a recent scandal had brought undesired attention to the athletic department. A story had ripped through the campus and the basketball team had made front-page headlines in the local newspaper. Part of that story had been about a player who kept his girlfriend locked in his apartment for a few days and apparently had beaten her, too, for good measure. He told the police they had disagreed about which movie to watch; she had gotten "mouthy." So he hit her and locked her in the apartment while he left to go to a party. The press was not good for the team or the campus and certainly not for the basketball coach, our own pretty-boy coach at the height of his stardom with his two-hundred-dollar coifs and his slick reputation.

Everything went downhill from there for the coach, but that's another story altogether. Suffice it to say we have a *new* basketball coach. A quick study, Matthew determined that player violence toward girlfriends was causing a lot of trouble for our team in the NCAA. A workshop on partnership violence was a sure cure. So the Troubling Violence Performance Troupe was dutifully contacted and an eight o'clock performance scheduled on an extraordinarily hot summer morning. A few coaches, we thought, and their assistants.

The troupe arrived at the athletic complex in different cars and congregated at the door. They knew less than Heather and I about this event, and we didn't know very much at all. We certainly knew about the accusations against the player for his treatment of his girlfriend—everyone did. They also knew that this man had been befriended and protected by our university president. Of course, the president had recently hung the player out to dry, quietly disengaging himself from the student who had spent a day riding his four-wheeler around the president's compound only to crash it into a tree with a nine-year-old boy on board. The president's spouse had visited the player in jail, causing even more consternation on campus and in the community. The whole thing just got messier and messier until the president suggested that his wife stay home and stop talking to the press. Damage control was most definitely failing.

So we huddled and wondered aloud about what we were getting ourselves into. One performer flatly wanted to finish her cigarette and go home. The vibes were all wrong, she declared, *especially* at eight o'clock in the morning. She hadn't had enough coffee for this. All the performers looked a bit shell-shocked; one person had performed only once or twice before, while another was doing his first performance. It was an important performance for this audience. We all knew that. That didn't help the performers, though. Perhaps they were feeling that coming had been a mistake.

But as usual, Heather was upbeat and encouraging. How bad could it be? I wasn't a big fan of sports or flashy coaches, and I was ready to throw the book at this player for his treatment of his girlfriend. I was especially concerned that the prosecutor couldn't get her to testify or bring charges. Although technically he could continue to prosecute without her, the chances of a solid conviction were slim unless she came forward. As so often happened, she declined the invitation to testify. Before the week was out, she had dropped out of school and had gone to live with relatives elsewhere.

We were reaching to open the building's enormous glass doors when we spied Matthew inside, walking toward us across the pale pink marble floors, gesturing for us to follow him to a room off the first white hallway. Not until he opened that second door for us did we realize that we were being herded into an enormous auditorium. There sat two hundred university coaches and assistant coaches slouched in red plush theater seats like pouting children. They had obviously been ordered to attend. It was mandatory. And it was deathly quiet.

But then we marched down the aisle, depositing the performers here and there in the crowd of black-and-gold athletic shirts and shorts. Heather walked across the stage and began to introduce herself and the troupe as she deftly located two chairs—our only props—and positioned them in the center of the stage.

Somehow Heather's strong, confident voice and the two chairs planted on the stage squarely in front of the athletic director (already visibly scowling) helped us all buck up and find our voices. I decided flatly *not* to look at the athletic director as I glanced around the room and caught the eye of our other performers. After that, it was easy. I moved onto the stage and began the performance of my story of working at the shelter. I told of how women stuffed their belongings into black plastic garbage bags, of their bruises and broken noses and their hopes for a meal and a clean bed. I told of how afraid the bulletproof windows and doors made me and of how I would watch through the blinds for potential trouble. And then I gestured to one of the empty chairs and told the story about a woman sitting in a car with her kids but no keys to the car and no way to go back into the house to retrieve them and leave. I told them I suspected the woman was dead and told them the empty chair was for her and all the other women who don't make it out in time.

And, like clockwork, the performers told their stories—of an aunt, a sister, and an abusive father. As we finished the stories and gathered on stage to sit and discuss the performances with our now shuffling, coughing, murmuring audience, we felt the charged air in the room. We recognized the closeted anger, the guilt in the four hundred eyes now poised on all of us—sitting ducks on a hostile stage.

I do not remember the exact questions asked, but I do recall that many audience members were defensive, argumentative, angered by the suggestion that men are abusive and violent. I was convinced they really had not been able to hear or listen to the stories because their defenses were up so high, their walls so thick and impenetrable. Except for some of the women coaches. There, we could see a difference. Some averted their eyes; some had very red faces; the discomfort level was extreme. But there were no tears in this room for the victims, no volunteer stories from audience members eager to share their own experiences. I watched the men cross and recross their legs, lean back and stretch their arms across the seats on both sides the way men do when they wish to intimidate. Their eyes stared hard. This would not be an easy discussion.

The athletic director sat up straight in his seat and looked at one female performer, who was at eye level sitting on the edge of the stage. "How do you feel coming here, telling these stories, performing for all of us? How do you feel up there?" His question was clearly a challenge. Did she feel superior? To them? Was she accusing him/them of crimes against women? What exactly did she think she was doing here, sitting in front of all of them?

"How do I feel?" she repeated, her voice quiet, weak, jagged. "I'll tell you how I feel. I feel very much afraid right now. I felt deep fear when I walked into this room of what I think are very angry men. I wanted to go home. I am *very* uncomfortable, and I do not like being here. I am afraid of all of you. That's how I feel." Her eyes never wavered. She held him in her gaze, a young woman half his age and less than half his weight. A student staring down the university athletic director. He coughed and looked away.

The rest of that discussion is a total blur for me. I do not remember the rest of the discussion, if there was one. I do not remember leaving the building, although Heather reminded me that two women came to talk to us as we left the double doors, thanking us and offering to give us their stories for the troupe. And I do recall the basketball coach following us out, making small talk. Was he feeling guilty? Did he want to look like the good guy here? Matthew crept out of the auditorium and met us at the doors, inviting us to escape. We did. We got into our cars and left, each of us alone with our own thoughts, our fears, and our revulsion at what we had just seen and experienced in the land of the Tigers.

*ELAINE and HEATHER write in their notebooks. HEATHER gets up as if to shake off a thought.*

**HEATHER**  Remember that ride after the Truman State performance?

**ELAINE**  God. It was like having all my kids and yours in the car all at once.

**HEATHER AND ELAINE** (*Both chant*)  "We want to go to Taco Bell!"

**HEATHER** (*laughing*)  "What?" It is after nine o'clock at night, and I am driving a van full of students home from a performance two hours away.

**ELAINE** (*laughing; talking over Heather's protests*)  "Tacos! Burritos! Diet Coke!"
"Diet Coke? No way, regular Coke!"

**HEATHER**  *That* was a heady night for all of us. They just couldn't stop laughing contagiously and poking each other like grade-schoolers. I remember grinning while I pulled up to the intercom. I tried to get the order right with all that giggling. Then we hit the highway. The faces of the audience we just left do not fade as slowly as the mile markers.

*As HEATHER stops reading aloud what she has just written about the work of the troupe, she stares at ELAINE through her dark glasses, realizing that Elaine is looking distressed.*

HEATHER   What's going on right now with you? Do you want to read what you've been writing?

*ELAINE wipes away tears as she begins to read her notebook.*

ELAINE   At first I could not tell her how my heart had burst when she read the piece she had written about loving our feet. So simple, I thought, to love our feet. Yet never in my life before this week had I pampered my feet. *Never.* I could see on the spa worker's face the challenge she saw when she uncovered my feet. Did I tell her how these feet had worked alongside my mother's feet in southern Missouri fields of cotton, corn, and beans? Would she have believed me that only fifty years ago these feet had walked with my brothers three miles to school and sat in rows of eight grades near a potbellied stove? I did not tell her that. I do not tell anyone that story, or how my dad refused to drive us to the back fields for our day labor or to care for the pigs in the closed-off woods a mile from the house or how he beat us with a belt till we crushed to the floor while our mother watched.

A friend recently told me about a young friend of hers whose boyfriend at first just seemed a bit bossy and overprotective but had recently began to hit her. She told me about how this woman's soon-to-be-husband knelt before his bride during their wedding and quietly washed her feet in a ritual of love and humility. How, I wondered, could a man who had washed his wife's feet turn to strike her? The obscenity of breaking that humble promise, above all else, somehow broke my heart at that moment.

"It's the feet," I confessed. "Somehow, what touched me the most and made me sad beyond words was the feet."

And then I went into the toilet and threw up, violently, until my stomach stopped hurting and my body shook—cold, clammy, and cleansed.

Is this what it means to "write the body?" Visceral, unarticulated, embodied response.

Somehow, in this moment, I was the audience member moved to tears, who feels in her own body the stories the performers tell. And the memory of violence in my own body and hers rings true. Memory crying for redemption.

ELAINE *exits stage left.*

HEATHER  Rejuvenation. That's what today has been for me. Quieting my mind. Feeling my limbs.

Refreshment.

No one tells you they are moving into the corners of your mind, weaving their cobwebs and blowing the dust bunnies around. But they come. They slide down your rain barrel and into your cellar door. And sometimes you need to tidy up a bit.

Rearrange.

Rediscover.

Waking up.

Sometimes things move too fast for me.

The world keeps getting faster and faster. And just because I can keep up doesn't mean I want to.

How do I slow down without having to be sick to do it?

If I don't nurture my creative soul, it doesn't go away, but just like so many diseases, it can lie dormant—be in remission. So the trick is to have my cancer in remission and my creativity out.

How do you live in short-term parking?

ELAINE *enters with a tray of food.*

HEATHER  I know I'll write more pages soon. The sunshine, the waterfall, the coffee are beckoning.

HEATHER *pulls up another chair, stretches out, and closes her eyes.*
ELAINE *takes a sip of coffee and begins to write. She looks up to share
her notes with the audience.*


ELAINE   One of my dear friends, a local minister, had been following the work of the troupe for months. She came to performances,
sitting in the back of the room, watching. She took in the stories and
the audience responses. She heard in the discussions echoes of stories
she heard nearly every day in her office—stories of unhappy, abused
wives struggling to understand the violence in their homes in terms of
their Christian faith. Other ministers were likely to tell the women,
"Go home and be a better wife." Or "Look deep inside yourself and
ask the question—what am I doing to provoke this man?" Or "Suffer
as Christ suffered. It is an honorable burden to bear." Or "Forgive as
Jesus forgave. Your rewards will be greater if you can forgive."

But as my friend listened to the stories of a husband's rages, his
tendencies to strike out at a moment's notice against his wife or one
of their children, his deep abusive moods, his constantly belligerent
tone and critical comments about how she looked, her dress, her
hair, her cooking, her housekeeping, she despaired that such ministe-
rial responses seemed trite, inadequate, wrong.

Could she counsel these women to leave? Could she suggest that
they complain to the police? Should she go to the prosecutor herself?
Talk to the abusers? There were no good models for responding to
these delicate situations.

Nor did she have any answers for the mothers who came to her
with the knowledge that their teenage daughters were already in
dangerous relationships with boys not even out of high school. She
listened to the stories of rages of jealousy, car windows broken with
angry fists, girls raped, beaten, and forced to give sexual favors to
other boys their own age. She pondered her responses and prayed for
guidance that made sense both in terms of her faith and in terms of
what she believed to be right and true—responses that would reflect
her often unspoken beliefs that were not always the same as those of
the church "fathers."

She talked to me. We had shared years of work together when I wrote books about women in ministry, when I tape-recorded nearly every sermon she preached, when I sat at the feet of twelve bold women and learned from them about being women ministers.

"Perhaps," she ventured, "perhaps the Troubling Violence Performance Troupe could come to our young women's Christian retreat this year. I think they need to hear those stories and talk abut partnership violence and how it might affect their lives and those of their friends. Somehow, these young girls think domestic violence is what happens to married people, like their parents and the neighbors."

Then, she wavered. Maybe not. Maybe it would not be appropriate. But six months later, we found ourselves in the rustic lodge of the midstate Christian retreat center, telling our stories for twenty-one young women, ages thirteen to twenty-one. I looked around at their eager, bored, curious faces as the performers began to tell the stories they had selected to tell for this group of young women who were also still girls. I recognized Katie, who at twenty-one had the mind of a thirteen-year-old but an adult body. A Down syndrome baby, she had already exceeded her life expectancy and wanted to move out of her childhood home and strike out on her own. She had landed a minimum-wage job at a local restaurant thanks to a friend of the family. But her parents were concerned about how easily someone could take advantage of her. She was technically an adult, they knew, but both birth control and an intimate relationship seemed to them beyond her keen. I wondered how these stories would fall on Katie's innocent ears. I could see my friend's concern, too, as Katie went around the room giving the other girls hugs, chattering to herself or to anyone who would listen.

I saw my daughters' faces reflected in those of the girls in this room. My youngest would have been aloof, quizzical, a bit unwilling to engage. My older daughter would have been eager to participate, to learn, to share. I saw my nieces' faces and reminded myself that perhaps Cynthia would not be dead now if she had heard a performance like this one or participated in a discussion that warned of the danger of young boys rebuffed. Not that I would have wanted Cynthia to be less independent, sure of herself, but maybe she would not have stopped her car when she saw him on the dark country overpass near her home, walking toward her car with a smile on his face and a gun in his pocket. Maybe she would not have smiled back and rolled down her window. *Maybe . . .*

That discussion was difficult. None of the girls had stories they were willing to share. If they or their mothers were being abused at home, they certainly could not say that in this setting with all their church girlfriends and the minister sitting only a few feet away. And they certainly could not voice their concerns about the boy who seemed interested but a bit too pushy, who only agreed to go to parties where his friends were or only "allowed" her to sit with his friends at lunch, who checked her cell phone for incoming and out-going calls and messages, who e-mailed her veiled threats and then claimed he was only joking—couldn't she take a joke? How could she possibly bring up his insistence on her oral favors in the car and his persistence in asking if she would "do" his best friend while he watched? Say that at a church retreat? No way.

As they sat, still as mice, eyes bright and averted, hands in their laps, uncomfortable, one troupe member told the story of a boy who stalked her and five years later picked her up, promising to take her home but raped her before he kicked her out of the car and called her a slut, a cunt, a bitch for even thinking she could just choose to leave him. Oh, and if she told anyone about this, he would go to her dad and tell him she asked for it. He would tell her *dad.* And, she knew, he would.

Impassively, they heard Catherine tell about moving in with her boyfriend only last year, realizing too late how cruel he could be. Her parents didn't even know she was living with him. How could she tell them? But finally, one night while he was out drinking with his friends, she took a chance. She called her parents to come get her. She told them only a tiny bit of her story; she did not have to explain very much. Her parents lived 250 miles away. It was 3:00 in the morning. At 6:30 A.M., they were at her door with a pickup truck.

They hugged her quickly and packed her things into the boxes they had thrown into the back, and they took her home with them. They never asked her a single question. She told them what she needed to and no more. They were her parents; she was their daughter. They loved her. It was as simple as that. It was enough.

We intentionally performed stories of younger women at this teenage girls' retreat. One story told of a woman who had gotten pregnant at sixteen and had two babies by eighteen, how she tried to make it on food stamps, how she had fallen for a guy who promised to take care of her and her children but instead hurt them every single day, how she lived for months in a women's shelter. These stories were of real young women, just like them, who had thought they were in love, who thought they had met their prince who would marry them and take care of them forever. They heard women's voices talking about the fairy tale gone wrong and the little things they had missed in their eagerness to have a cool boyfriend or to fit in with a certain crowd, trying to please everyone—except themselves.

But they also heard strong stories of these and other women who made different choices, who made mistakes but then broke free, who said, "No," who resisted pleasing others. They heard stories of young women who went back to school even after having children, who got their GEDs and college degrees, who spoke proudly of what they had accomplished and how their girls were strong, getting older, and were a bit mouthy even, not interested in pleasing others, content to be proud of themselves.

Mostly, I think, the girls in that room on that early evening were overwhelmed. What in the world should they do or think about this information? How could they play shuffleboard and card games, drink Coca-Cola and eat pizza after *this?* I could tell that my friend, their minister, was thinking the same thing.

We need not have worried. As we left, the audience transformed itself instantly into a gaggle of giggling girls, moving chairs for games, playing the out-of-tune piano in pairs, and dragging out food and drinks. There might not be any processing tonight.

Months later, as my minister friend and I walked along the boardwalk in a nearby river town, catching up on our lives, trying to remember what we had not yet shared with each other because of the strain of our too-busy lives, she remembered to tell me about the effects of that evening. Nothing happened at first, she said, but a while later, she got a phone call from one girl and an e-mail from another. Just the previous week, a girl had sat in her office and talked for an hour about a boy she thought might be abusive. Another girl told her how the performance troupe stories had given her the courage to break up with her boyfriend and how much happier she was to have gotten her life back and to be with her friends. A mom came in to talk about how her daughter had, out of the blue, begun discussing with her parents her fears about a boy who was stalking her. What should she do, she asked them? They hugged her and told her they would figure it out together.

Me? I'm still the pessimist. Every time I pick up the newspaper and read about a girl's murder, a woman's death, I say to my husband, "Just wait. In a few days, we'll learn it was her boyfriend or her husband who did it." He thinks I'm a bit jaded. He's right. I am.

But in a few days, he sees the reports, and he has to acknowledge I was right all along. I see this stuff too much. I have heard too often the possessive justification, "If I can't have her, no one can." Women die every day at the hands of men who say they love them.

I hope my friend invites us back this year to the young women's Christian retreat. This time I will know that even though their eyes are cautious and their faces impassive, they are listening. They can definitely hear us.

HEATHER *nods and begins to read from her notebook.*

HEATHER  The invitation for the troupe to fly to a southern university for a paid performance was exciting in many ways. The troupe would travel for the first time with all expenses paid. Our work had been solicited by a college department at a southern school by a woman who had seen us perform at a narrative conference earlier that year in Boston. I was eager to go—a dear friend from my childhood lived in the area and I knew she and her mother would come to the performance. Little did I know that they would also provide us with plush accommodations and warm hospitality.

Even though it was in the middle of a semester, we had three performers who could take two days out of their busy schedules to travel with us and perform. Elaine and I also juggled our teaching, our departmental duties, and our home responsibilities for a two-day midweek trip to the South.

It all seemed so right.

This is the part where you, the reader, might say "Uh, oh," as if anticipating that I am about to say that then it all went wrong.

But, no, that didn't happen.

We had an excellent trip, and we were greeted with genuine hospitality by my friend's mother and her entire family. In fact, we feared our students might just refuse to leave.

The storytelling professor who had invited us after seeing us previously was a pleasure to meet. She coordinated our stay with grace and style. We ate well; we always knew where we needed to be. Her enthusiasm for our work was wonderful.

For this event, we performed in a large space—a rectangular room in the student union with large, disconcerting columns throughout the room that blocked audience members' views. The acoustics were poor, so they asked us to use microphones. We were uncomfortable with this set-up because our kind of performance really doesn't lend itself to mics and mic stands and electrical cords snaking across the stage in all directions. Reminding ourselves of our steady commitment to flexibility at all costs and in any space, however, we positioned ourselves and began the performance.

At the outset, I introduced a dedicated therapist from the local counseling center who brought handouts for the audience. I suggested that anyone needing to talk with her after the performance and discussion or later in the week could do so.
She was eager to help.

I introduced Elaine, who performed her piece about working in the shelter and hearing women's stories there. The three student performers shared powerful, poignant stories; some of them were our own stories, and some were of women we loved and for whom we feared.

And as with every performance, after sharing the narratives, we all gathered on the stage in our horseshoe pattern and sat facing our audience. I asked the question so common to us by then—What did you just hear?

And we waited.

I looked across the three hundred or so faces in that room and told myself to wait calmly. Here we were in a different state. A different culture. Worlds away from our own comfort zone.

We did not have to wait long before hands began to shoot up all over the room. The storyteller professor leapt into action with a microphone, and we felt the high of a conversation with the audience for almost two hours. It was as though a dam had broken. These people wanted to talk.

The conversation included everything from questions about restraining orders to personal accounts of intimate violence in the audience members' lives. Many were visibly shaken, with tears in their eyes as they rose from their chairs to comment, to share, to inquire, to grieve. One young man shook with emotion as he told us and the audience how important this work was for him. Afterward, I talked with him and he told me about his cousin who had been murdered by her boyfriend. It had been years long past, but he had never forgotten the pain.

The trip was long and exhausting but well worth it. The audience had embraced our work, and we felt confident in our success. A talk-back session with the professor the next morning further energized us as she articulated the power of the performance, which she and her students had felt viscerally.

*Both women pause from their furious writing and alternate reading as they listen to the strains of Bob Marley wailing out the lyrics to the reggae classic "Survivor."*

**HEATHER**  On the plane ride home, I remembered a woman who stood at the end of the performance and asked us why we had not talked about the identifiable patterns in the well-known "cycles of violence." I told her that notions of a cycle can trap women's experiences into violent scripts that they feel are already written—with no escape. Elaine and the other troupe members also spoke about getting rid of notions that became self-fulfilling prophecies. We also discussed the possibility that violence and abuse come in many different guises—What happens if your experience of abuse never fits the prescribed patterns? Do you question whether it really is abuse? Do others judge your experiences as not authentically abusive? What are the dangers of published, defined cycles and checklists of "Ten Clues to Tell If Your Boyfriend May Become Violent?" The woman who had asked the question seemed dissatisfied with our discussion and sat down.

I fastened my seatbelt, making a mental note about the charged air during that final exchange. Six hours of driving, eight hours in the airport, flying time, commuting home, walking with our bags after nearly three hours at the performance and only five hours of sleep, we returned exhausted to our campus and home lives.

Exhausted.

Overwhelmed.

Proud.

Energized with the thought that our work was worth it, was valued, no matter how much our households and teaching schedules had been overturned. Definitely worth it.

Only a few days later, a letter came from the storytelling professor who had invited us. She had been so pleased; she thanked us profusely. And she wanted to share with us how a student who had not talked a great deal before had told her class about how powerful the performance had been for him, a child of an abusive household.

All good.

Now, reader, your feelings about something amiss looming may emerge again. And here you are right.

A few days later, the women's studies group that was to pay

for our trip sent us a letter. It was *not* complimentary. The letter pointed out that because this southern campus was located in one of the wealthiest counties in the state, the group's leaders found it completely inappropriate that we performed stories about women living in trailer courts and living in poverty. The letter reiterated the complaint that we had not addressed the published information about the "cycles of violence," as they had expected. Furthermore, they complained, they had anticipated a more sophisticated staged production, and for the amount of money they were paying, they had expected us to "entertain" the audience better and for a longer time. They asked for their money back. The letter informed us that they would not be sending the agreed-upon further payment for our services.

We were floored.

The professor who invited us was appalled.

My department's dedicated fiscal officer pointed out that we had a contract (thank goodness), and she would see that it was properly executed.

The graduate student financial person who felt that we had promised more and more appropriately "class-based" performances continued to withhold our payments.

I wondered what aspect of women's studies she was studying.

I wrote an e-mail that stated emphatically, we came; we performed; we gave our work and the time and energy of two professors and three graduate students committed to ending violence against women. We had, indeed, fulfilled our contract.

I wrote that I could not continue to participate in this ridiculous e-mail correspondence. I was scheduled to go into the hospital for a bilateral mastectomy at the end of the week.

We will not be shamed by men.

We will not be shamed by women.

We will not be shamed by race.

We will not be shamed by class.

We will not be shamed by gender.

We will not be shamed by religion.

We know who we are, and we know we touch people's lives. The audiences always tell us so.

Excuse me. I am off to fight for my life.

Please send payment due. Now.

ELAINE *nods in remembrance of the events of that trip as well as her acknowledgment of* HEATHER's *current battle with cancer. After a pause,* ELAINE *begins to read from her notebook again.*

ELAINE Frankie was one of the core faithful. We weren't quite sure why, but she was passionate about the troupe work from the very beginning. She came to every performance and was openly critical of those not as dedicated. For the first few performances, Frankie chose a story out of my book—a story told to me by a young woman who had made a critical mistake in marrying a man she thought she loved. He ran over her sister's dog with his pickup truck and broke down the door of her sister's house trying to reach her after she had left. He always told her he just "went crazy" because he loved her so much. If she was out of his sight or he didn't know where she was or who she might be with, he said again, it just made him "crazy." She wondered if this kind of jealousy was true love; perhaps it was something else. Once he followed her car when she gave a ride home to a male coworker. He approached her car at a stop sign and put his hand through the window on her side; then he ordered her to take the man home as he followed behind. He quit his job so that he could hang out at the convenience shop where she worked. He would glare at men who came in to buy gas and cigarettes and who flirted with her. After they were married, he forced her to quit her job, allowing her to return to work only at desperate intervals when his unemployment checks ran out. He refused to stay home with the kids, so she never could work more than a few weeks at a time, relying on friends, her mother, and her sister to help with the children. She moved into the shelter when she realized that her husband had begun to hit her kids, too. Eventually, she feared he was or soon would be sexually abusing her seven-year-old daughter. As

Frankie finished the narrative and stared off into space with exactly the expression of resignation I had seen on the woman in the shelter who had told me her story, I knew just how close to reality this performance was and that Frankie already knew, inherently or from experience, the woman's pain and her daily suffering.

But then she began to explore a different story, one about a woman she knew. Frankie was never sure about the ethics of performing her friend's very personal, private story in public venues, but she eventually performed the story at many of the troupe's performances. It rang true, and audiences responded to it. It gripped listeners because it felt so real.

It was real.

When we began the troupe with only a handful of stories that had been given to me at the shelter, we really had no vision of how we might acquire new stories. Little did we suspect that audience members would offer us their stories. Even less did we realize that the members of our troupe would begin telling their own stories of stalking boyfriends, rapists, and abusive live-ins. Troupe members came to realize, as Frankie had, that they had to tell their stories and those of their best friends, their sisters, their mothers. They knew it would never get easy.

It should never be easy.

HEATHER *reads from her notebook.*


HEATHER   Ducks fly overhead. The music from the Parrot Bar is ebullient—a Bob Marley CD again. The two men working there are friendly in their flowered shirts, conversing in thick African accents, humming along, "We are the survivors."

I wonder if my feet are getting sunburned. They are the only part of my body exposed. I cannot help but want to wiggle my toes in the cool breeze as I look out at the lake. More birds. Light music.

I don't want to die soon.

I don't think I will.

I think the cancer's gone, and I've worked to get rid of the toxins in my body.

Slowing down has been good for me. I plan on staying with this plan this summer. I don't have to do anything I do not want to do. Nice.

Projects—script with Mary; book with Elaine; letters of recommendation. Being with Tricia and Ellie. Maybe we can go over to Elaine's and hang out. The girls could read or write or play in the yard. Elaine and I could write.

We could get work done together.

We can weave our lives together.

We are friends.

ELAINE Kandi never spoke in class. True, she could have inserted herself into the class more, but I could also have tried to pull her into the discussions. At least for a semester or two, we were but ships passing in the academic world. Then Kandi took the ethnography and performance course Heather and I were teaching. She was eager to experience how ethnography and performance might work together, eager to perform, eager to learn about Dwight Conquergood, Carolyn Ellis, Ron Pelias—authors we had not encountered in the ethnographic writing course, not because their books did not have *ethnography* in their titles but more because we had been reading folklore and anthropology works. Now we could read scholars trained in performance studies; we were all learning together and loving it. The connections made sense.

Performance, recognized in folklore studies since the 1960s as the understanding that all folk artists—from chair makers to storytellers—are actually "performing" the traditional knowledge they carry and share with their local audiences. But this concept came alive when we asked our students to perform their fieldwork experiences and to perform their main informants.

Kandi's first performance fit her to a T. We found ourselves chuckling a bit in recognition as she marched into the room in true sorority attire, hair and makeup perfect, heels and hemline as per specifications. Her voice was a little loud, not brassy, just bossy, but in a good way. She was, she told us briskly, the Greek life coordinator, and we were parents visiting the MU campus. She was clear, efficient, cheery, and convincing as she assured us, all a bit nervous about sending our seventeen-year-old daughters into her care. But she was convincing as she assured us and placated our fears. She had *handouts!* She had posters of smiling faces, charts of sorority academic successes, award winners, community service. She told us about curfews and rules and standards and rules and requirements and rules and—

We listened, amazed, assured our baby girls would, in fact, be OK with Kandi at the helm.

And, she smiled broadly, pure white teeth dazzling us, our girls would also have a new family in the sorority of their choice. They would have new big sisters who would guide them, listen to them, protect their backs. The big sisters had already been around the block a year or two and knew the ropes. They would teach our daughters how to survive on a large midwestern campus with nearly twenty thousand young (horny, no doubt we were all thinking) men. The bonds the women made in the Greek system would last a lifetime. Sorority sisters never, ever let these friendships die. They are family. They had shared too much; the bonds were that deep. Flashing her bright smile again and tossing her shining hair, Kandi asked if we had any questions. Stunned, we did not.

Several weeks later, Kandi performed her second assignment, a college student whose boyfriend was in a fraternity. Although she was not a sorority woman herself (her parents couldn't afford the astronomical fee to get her into the house), the student nevertheless spent a great deal of time in the frat house with Aston, her boyfriend. She told how the men there greeted her when she arrived: "How you doing, Tits?" Or "Here comes Aston's bitch." Or "Come over here, Sweetie, and give me a blow job before you go up to service Aston." She talked about how hard it was to hear this banter about her body and the assumptions that if she was in the frat house, she was, in fact, a slut. She was certain that they didn't even know her name, nor did they care to learn it.

The woman complained to Aston, who laughed and told her that she was being way too sensitive. "That's what frat men do," he assured her. "It's who they are. That's what they learn in the Greek system. It's normal." If she didn't like it, Aston suggested, perhaps she just shouldn't come to the frat house anymore. Obviously, this was her problem, not theirs.

She was not satisfied with this solution. She began to think about the ramifications of a frat culture that institutionalized and normalized learned behavior of a culture of male violence and abuse of women. In the frat house, women were not really human, they were objects, body parts, and sexual machines: cunts, whores, sluts, bitches, tits, butts, brainless, cocksuckers, motherfuckers. The list seemed endless as she began to listen with newly tuned (angry) ears.

One night, Kandi told us in a conspiratorial voice, she found a young woman crying in a room of the frat house. She worried that the woman had been insulted. The story, after she got the woman to talk to her, was far, far worse than words of abuse and slander. The woman feared that she had been raped, perhaps repeatedly by different men. She had vague memories of a hazing ritual in which she had to "suck the cocks" of all the senior frat men, one after the other. She remembered getting drunk and feeling sick. She remembered hard hands pressed against her head, pushing her head into yet another penis standing ready for her to "service." Their faces were hidden from view; she could see only the lower half of each man's body.

Kandi asked which fraternity had such a hazing ritual that would include the sorority women. Through her sobs and tears, the woman sitting on the dirty, rumpled bed in that disgusting room said that it wasn't the fraternity hazing her, it was her sorority. This was one of the things you had to do to stay in the house. They all had to do it. Afterward, it was part of what bonded them so tightly together. They had all been there, done that. Kandi could hardly breathe.

"There's more," the woman whispered. She told about a room in the basement of this frat house, a room with nothing in it except a mattress on the floor and cans of spray paint all over the place. Every frat member who brought a woman down to this room and fucked her on that mattress got to paint his name on the wall. The room was, the woman told Kandi, covered floor and ceiling with the names of fine, upstanding frat men bragging to their peers of their sexual prowess.

The woman whispered. "I was drunk. I think I was drugged. I really don't know all that happened last night. Can you help me?"

When Kandi confronted the frat men about this woman's story and what had apparently happened in the frat house the night before, they issued a collective sigh. "It wasn't rape," one claimed. "She didn't say 'No' when he took off her clothes on the mattress. In fact, she didn't say anything because she was probably passed out. That's not rape. She'd been making out with him all night. She was drunk. She passed out. That's not rape."

"It's not rape, is it?"

Kandi leaned over, her elbows on her knees, looking straight at us, her audience.

"Is it?"

"Is it?"

Her question hung in the room. Then she got up and walked out the door.

We asked Kandi if she would join the Troubling Violence troupe and perform her story as she had just performed it in the class. She was quick to agree, with all of us knowing that there were serious implications in this story about the Greek system on our own campus. We knew there were great concerns about sorority and Greek life in general nationwide. But Kandi was ready to take on the Greek system. She didn't care if doing so was politically correct or not, and neither did we. Her story set the stage for discussions of verbal abuse of women, for the objectification of women's and young girls' bodies, for the normalizing not only of abuse but also of a learned male culture of violence against women.

When Kandi performs her story, the effect is disturbing—as it should be.

Her story always elicits a response from the audience. It serves our purposes well. We've been asking how violence against women begins, how men learn to demean, despise, and degrade women. It is an easy step, we posit, from four years of this kind of intense "training" in the frat house to a lifetime of violence and abuse.

Think about it: Most of these handsome, well-bred, well-educated fraternity men will stand beside their new brides within a few years of graduation and pledge to love, honor, and respect them as their wives. How, we ask, can such men erase those recent four years? Is it any wonder that they can slip easily into calling women sluts, bitches, whores when they disagree with their husbands or when life becomes rocky, as it invariably does? Why wouldn't he slap her, even though at the beginning he could see no connection at all to the women who came to the frat house every night, who offered blow jobs, who got drunk and passed out on the mattress in the basement. They would not and did not marry any of *those* women. No, they would say, they married pretty sorority women, good girls, or women from back home, virgins who were quiet, well dressed, and pretty and who would be the mothers of their children. These were two completely different worlds. The one had nothing to do with the other.

Blindness is bliss.

It's still rape.

*It is.*

We turn to the audience of both men and women: Even in your own home six years later, it's still abuse; it's still violence; it's still rape. You have been trained as well.

You do not respect yourself.

You do not respect women.

You have been trained to demean and despise women. Women are only walking body parts available for your stares, your evaluation, your pleasure.

Those women are your wives now.

They are.

And they are damaged goods, just like you are.

In fact, you did the damage.

Now you are married. Where else can you focus the anger, the frustrations, the hatred of your job, the pressures to make more money, to buy a house, a nicer car, to dress well and travel to resorts in exotic places? Perhaps it is her fault. She is, after all, just a bitch.

It is still abuse.

It is still violence.

It is still rape.

And it is always wrong.

For the next two years, Kandi performed the story she had developed in our course. Students on campus and in the Greek system heard her tell this story; faculty and other students in classes heard this story; athletes heard this story; and participants at conferences near and far heard this story.

"Fraternity Narrative," as told by Kandi
I can still remember my first frat party, freshman year. People were everywhere—scattered on the lawn, in the house, on the balcony, in the basement—walking around with their little plastic cups of beer from the keg and music blaring so loud you couldn't hear the person standing next to you. And the only reason I got in is because my best friend, Erica, was dating this guy, Jake, one of the guys in the house. She had dated another guy, Mike, from the same house, but he was older and transferred a while back. In fact, I can remember very vividly the first time Jake introduced Erica to his friends in the house because one of them came up and said, right in front of her, "So Erica, what does Jake's dick taste like?" And I remember thinking, "OK, maybe he just said it because he was drunk. I don't know." But I started spending a lot of time over there because of Erica and began to notice that these kinds of comments were actually pretty frequent. I mean, it seemed like every time I came over, I was greeted with "What's up, Slut?"

or "What's up, Boobs?" It was never by my name. I don't think some of them even knew my name.

I can remember walking down the hall to Jake's room one time and this whole room full of guys was just chanting over and over again, "Blonde hair, big tits, dumb, and slutty"—the kind of girl they were looking for. They said they were joking, but no, seriously, that's what they wanted. It just seemed like every conversation I engaged in always turned sexual in some way. I mean, I remember one time I just asked a guy to hand me my backpack and he said, "Well, give me a quickie and then maybe I'll think about it." Or one time Jake was working on a paper and one guy came in and said, "What are you writing a paper on, Jake, getting a blow job?" I mean, everything was sexual. Most of the rooms were covered in posters of half-naked women, and there were porn movies and dirty magazines lying on the table. Most of the time Erica and I would sit around and listen to them swap sex stories or tell sex jokes. Looking back on it, I can remember the guys that didn't have a story or a joke to tell were called some pretty degrading things—you know, they were a "fucking pussy" or a "faggot."

Not only did I hear a lot of things, but I also saw a lot of things. One night, we came back to the house and there were a bunch of people standing outside someone's door, and when Jake asked what was going on, they said Jim was fisting some girl they called "Fatso" and they were watching through the hole in the door. That same night, one member went around looking for a can of spray paint because he had sex in some room in the basement that has a doorway and no door because if you have sex in there, you get to spray paint your name on the wall. You would think that would be disgusting enough, but it also turns out that another member was so drunk that he peed on a woman while she was sleeping and they started joking about how she liked "golden showers" or liked to be peed on during sex, which turned into she also likes it when guys come all over her face or chest or whatever. I don't know how these stories get

started, but whenever I showed a sign of disgust, they said they
were just joking. This woman stopped coming over because of
the rumors, and then they said that if she couldn't take a joke,
then she was a dumb bitch anyway.

I think they may have taken some jokes too far, though, like
when Erica told me about one of the girlfriends in the house
being humiliated. She and her boyfriend, another member of
the house, were drunk and had sex or whatever and had passed
out when the roommate unlocked the door and came in. He
thought it would be funny to gather other people and arrange
her in different positions while she was naked and take pictures.
They sprinkled tortilla chips on her ass because they said it was
hairy so they started calling her hairy ass. They didn't want to
look at it. They hung up the pictures like a week later, and the
boyfriend was pissed, but they said they didn't care. It didn't
matter. They said she wasn't cute. She was fat. I don't know,
it just seemed like they didn't take to girlfriends very well.
Another girlfriend that Erica came to be close with doesn't come
over anymore either because the guys told her she was fucking
annoying. They said she looked funny because her eyes were
sort of cross-eyed so they started calling her googly-eyed bitch.
In fact, they even made a sign one day that said we cannot allow
Rick in this room because he'll bring that fucking annoying
bitch with him. She saw it and started crying. Rick broke up
with her shortly after. They said it was just a joke, but the guy
who made the poster said he hated that girl. She was over too
much. And I know Erica herself was embarrassed a few times,
like when some of the guys told her that they saw her having sex
with Jake or heard it going on or knew it was going on, or they
claimed Jake told them things about their sex life.

One time, they came in and sang a song while she was
sleeping with Jake in his loft, something about her being a virgin
until she met her fraternity man and he fucked her. I don't know.
I know she was pretty embarrassed, though. And I remember
I asked Jake one time if he'd seen other guys in the house have

sex, and he said he'd seen it in just about every room of the house, but when you live in such close quarters, it's really not embarrassing or uncomfortable—for him, anyway. In fact, he laughed and told me it's encouraged. Now, I don't know exactly what it is that's encouraged or why, but one of our mutual friends won't really come over anymore because she was friends with a lot of guys in a different house and she had to crash over there one night and she woke up in the middle of the night with some guy on top of her with his hands down her pants. I know she was pretty scared. You know, I have heard a lot of stories, a lot of jokes over the years because I was around so much because of Erica, but I can still remember one of the guys talking to me at one of the many parties I went to and he asked me, "What if a girl is drunk but she tells you she wants to have sex with you, but when you go upstairs, she passes out. Is it still OK to have sex with her? I mean, since she said she wanted to?" Now, I've learned what a strange sense of humor some of these guys have, so I'm sure he was just joking.

I mean, he was joking, wasn't he?

Wasn't he?

Wasn't he?

*HEATHER turns to ELAINE to ask a question.*

**HEATHER** That reminds me, how did you get Annie's story?

**ELAINE** Annie was not in the course Heather and I taught together. But she had been a student of mine years before, taking courses with me on women's literature and women's folklore and feminist theory. It had been a delight to watch her grow and mature as a person, as a writer, as someone who was becoming very sure of herself as a woman and eventually openly a lesbian. But those changes were gradual, and she seemed to develop smoothly and consistently. I didn't worry that I didn't hear from her; students come and go in my life all the time. In fact, it's a kind of sad reality. I stay here and teach, write, and raise my family, and students move in and then out of my life, each one affecting me differently and some affecting me more than others. Annie knew she was special. We had truly connected in my classes, and I knew somehow that she would get in touch again someday.

Eventually, she did, but the e-mail was hardly what I had expected. She began her message by telling me that she had bought my book, *Women Escaping Violence*, and had begun reading it. But she had had to stop reading it, she said, because at one particular point in the book, she was taken aback by the language I was using to describe different kinds of violence against women's bodies. There was, she said, one sentence in chapter 2 that caught her up short. We corresponded for some time about her reading my book, her discomfort with what I had written. She wrote her response as a journal piece that eventually became her performance for the troupe. It took her some time to write the piece, but one day, she read her narrative to me in my office. I cried. How could I have known? We invited Annie to join the troupe and perform this story—her story.

"What's in This for Me?," as told by Annie
You know, I believe in the mission of this project. I really do. To get on stage and tell the stories. The subtitle of Elaine's book is "Empowerment through Narrative." Healing through telling. But what if that doesn't work for me? Then what do I get out of this? I mean, what? That I tell my story and some of you may understand? That I'll get through to one of you somehow and someone out there will feel inspired to think of volunteering for a week or two? I mean, if we're successful tonight, one of you'll be there to listen when someone you know asks you for understanding. These issues will affect you in your lifetime. But, I repeat, what do I get out of this? How do I benefit?

In this world we live in, this Judeo-Christian society I grew up in, "To err is human; to forgive, divine." Fuck that. I don't want to forgive him. I don't want to forgive my parents either. Or my ex-girlfriend for never believing or supporting me the way she should have and the way I needed her to. Or any of the numerous friends and mentors and adults I've told who ignore it, scoff it off, don't believe me, have told me to forgive.

And now I'm guessing you're all thinking the same thing, the same old bullshit about forgiveness and how I must just not be far enough along in the healing process, and to truly move on I need to accept what happened, talk about it, tell the stories, and then forgive.

I repeat: Fuck that. I hate him.

You know, I started to read Elaine's book. I joined this group, I got a full-time job working for social justice, and I started to read Elaine's book.

After the poem, after the prologue, after the intro, past chapter 1, I got all the way into the second chapter, sixty-three pages of emotionally draining and terribly triggering violence against women. I stopped reading in chapter 2, at the section called "Some of the Hard to Hear Facts." I even have the sentence memorized: "They are beaten, abused, and violated by the men they cohabitate with—fathers, uncles, sometimes brothers, and, most often, by their spouses and partners."

I ask you again—what do I get out of this? Is one of you gonna understand? Is one of you gonna stop the nightmares? The oh-so-real nightmares that literally jerk me awake—his wiry, red leg hair scratching my sides as he holds me down; hearing the wire hanger clang against the back of the bathroom door when he comes in and I'm in the bathtub; the desperation in his heavy-breathing voice as he pleads for "my pussy" and I fail again at fighting him off—one of you is gonna stop that from catching me off guard, stop it from keeping me up at night, stop all of it?

No. No.

If Elaine, the author of the fucking book, if she doesn't even get it, how are any of you supposed to?

What am I getting out of this?

Yes. Yes, sometimes brothers.

But, apparently not "sometimes" enough. Not "sometimes" enough to be listed like all the rest.

No. Not me. Not only am I one of those women who's been abused, who's been molested, who's been sexually assaulted, who's a survivor of incest, but I'm set apart from the rest. I only happen "sometimes." I get to be included in the list but differentiated one step further from the world—marginalized within my marginalized group—by the addition of a well-placed degree modifier. "Sometimes brothers."

Sometimes! As if you guess it's possible, but you've never actually heard of any real cases. As if it's just too terrible to believe and can't be real. As if it's not my life. As if I don't have to go back at holidays and the worst part isn't even being there—I dealt with it my whole childhood, I deal with it every day. I've got the panic attack on the cold tile of my grandparents' bathroom floor down—it's the judgments I get for not liking my family, for not being excited it's Christmas. The judgments passed because I don't try to just work it out. Whatever it is, it's family, you've only got one, right? Again, "To err is human; to forgive, divine." People everywhere feel the right to tell me about my family and how I should deal with them.

One of my friends told me that she doesn't like her mom either; you just deal. There are lots of catchphrases: "No family's perfect." "I wasn't friends with my brother when we were younger, but now I tell him everything." "Oh, you know how older brothers are: so protective." "Family is the most important thing in the world." "Family will always be there for you." Or my personal favorite, "I love you like a sister."

You're never gonna know what happened. I am not on this stage to tell my story or to get it all out or to cry for help. I don't need to try again to tell someone else and be misunderstood. I don't want to tell anyone else ever again. Why? To have people be frightened of me and my past? What would I get out of it?

I eventually picked up Elaine's book again. Not that section, but I would flip through and read, trying to learn, trying to get a better performance. Trying to heal.

Turns out there's a whole section on silence and women who can never get their stories out. That part gave me hope. Maybe I'm not alone. Maybe none of us that fit so well into the "Incest and Early Childhood Molestation" section have an easy time telling specifics, telling at all.

I don't know why I keep talking, or why I try to trust people, why I keep picking up Elaine's book, or even why I keep performing. But I know I'm still not telling.

What would I get out of that?

Perhaps a year after she performed this story, we asked for Annie's permission to include it in this book. She agreed, telling me in an e-mail, "I remember all of this pretty well as it was such a huge step for me in the ongoing healing process for me." We would like to believe that Annie got something out of doing this after all. In fact, I know she did. She told me far more in that e-mail than I feel comfortable sharing here. But there is no doubt telling even this much of her story began the healing process for her—as it has done for so many of us.

# Act II

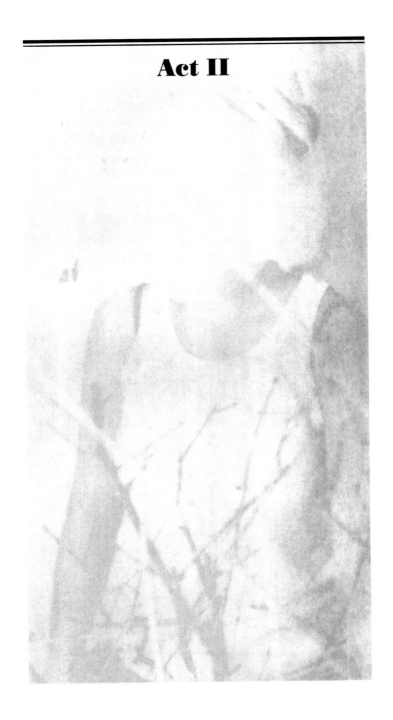

# Writing the Body

*Lights up on two women at a table; the sounds and reflection of a lake surround them on stage. The table is loaded with books, food, drinks, and cell phones (for emergencies back home). One shares her written notes with the audience while the other one continues to write.*

HEATHER   I am feeling bossy right now.
Sometimes I get bossy.
Elaine lets me.
I hope it isn't too much.

*ELAINE looks up and addresses the audience.*

ELAINE *(pointing to Heather)*   "Write about your body," she says.
Hmmm...

*HEATHER looks up from her notebook, laughs, and tries to defend herself to the audience.*

HEATHER   But she wanted a prompt!

*ELAINE returns to her notebook.*

HEATHER   I like to just write and fill up the page. I like to have conversations on the page. I don't always think about the words that follow. *[gestures to ELAINE]* But she's writing about her body. Maybe I should write about mine.
My feet feel fantastic. But my hand is already cramping. I feel quiet. Calm? Unsure about that. I don't know if I know calm.

I am sitting here at the lake, and it is gorgeous. There's a waterfall on my left and the blue waters of the Lake Ozark just beyond a hut labeled the Parrot Bar—"wasting away in Margaritaville." No one is in the swimming pool. My back is relaxed, and my legs are light. My chest feels loose, and breathing is easy.

Deep breath in.

Deep breath out.

Interlopers at one o'clock. If I don't look, maybe they'll disappear. Moving into two o'clock view and then walking by, they laugh. Head down, I ignore them and do not smile. I'm not here to make friends. I am here with my friend Elaine. We're here to write. We're here to breathe. We're here to find calm if it lurks nearby.

Goals include many things: looking at our work, really looking at what needs to be finished, what needs to be written. Divide and conquer. Elaine pulls out her notebook about our book. We started that book of plans before I got sick. Most of the troupe's work was accomplished before I got sick. I'm not sick now, and I'm not going to let work make me sick again. So, write your body. Just do it.

# Violence against
# Our Bodies

ELAINE  The way our bodies are violated is without a doubt a "troubling" kind of violence, especially for women. Heather and I talk a lot about how we sandwich writing and teaching, thinking and reading, between children's Halloween costumes and parades, softball games, gymnastics meets, finding money for new uniforms, shoes, clothes, tournaments, and all the stuff that we do as mothers and what we do as partners and spouses. It's all good, we agree, it's just sometimes too much when it's added onto or done in conjunction with faculty meetings; student dissertations and defenses; meetings, meetings, and more meetings; forms to fill out; duties all over campus and at conferences thousands of miles away. Heather believes she got cancer because she wasn't taking good care of herself. Some days I believe that is totally possible; other days I cannot admit it is true because then all mothers doing what we are trying to do would have cancer, right? Why does one body succumb and another resist? Or maybe the violence just appears in different guises—cancer, kidney stones, arthritis, fibromyalgia, mental illness, paranoia, schizophrenia.

Today we got pedicures, taking care of our feet. At this moment, my body is not in pain; I feel light and still, at peace.
But most days, I think I have ulcers, and I know I have serious, debilitating, degenerative arthritis. I have a history of ulcers that began nine months after I married my first husband at age twenty. My stomach hurts; it feels like it's tied in knots; food doesn't digest well; I hold myself very, very tightly sometimes just to keep things under control.

My fingers look like those of a ninety-year-old woman. If you don't believe me, look at them. Nodes the size of golf balls.

X-rays of my feet last week revealed I have the same thing going on in the bones of my feet, making those long walks on the trail excruciating. I'll get orthotics soon. Sounds like I'm a really old woman. I'm actually not. I just turned sixty, though, so the reality of age is hitting me pretty hard. "Oh, you don't look sixty," everyone tells me, beaming with their good news. But that doesn't really help so much because my body tells me daily and in many ways that I am indeed sixty and getting older by the minute. I try to exercise, but pain is a daily interruption; my sleep is also in fits and starts. The arthritis in my back has degenerated some of the disks to the point that they rub bone on bone at some of the joints and send sharp sciatic pain down my legs. I wake up gasping. But if I shift a bit to one side or the other, the pain subsides, and I can go back to sleep, at least for a while.

My friends are all complaining about symptoms of menopause. For me, those have been the normal, the even tolerable, parts of aging. I'm not certain, but I think that all those years working in the fields when I was ten, fifteen, even nineteen, before I married (disastrously) before my twentieth birthday, I ruined my body. I chopped weeds out of bean fields so large I could not see the borders of the fields in any direction in the sandy Mississippi delta flatland where I grew up. And, I spent my fall and winter weekends and vacations chopping cotton, then picking the cotton, and finally in the deep cold of December bolling the cotton. I worked alongside my mother and sometimes my father and brothers, picking the white gold out of sharp, thorny bolls and dragging a canvas bag behind that could weigh as much as eighty-five pounds to the truck and up on the weighing hook to be weighed and then dumped onto the mass of white fluffy clouds already in the truck. We got $3.25 per one hundred pounds of clean cotton picked. We had contests to see who could pick the most in a long, weary day. Mom and I could barely pick two hundred pounds, but my father and brothers often could top three hundred. We even got cotton vacations from school in the fall and winter to pick the cotton and then to boll it in December, which meant we put on heavy canvas gloves and stripped the cotton stalks, bolls and all, and stuffed that ugly, dirty, wet, cold, thorny mass into our sacks that we dragged once again to the weighing hook. Unlike the fluffy stuff we picked in the fall that went to the mills for the creation of lovely cotton fabrics, this mess went to the gin and was turned into oils and other industrial uses I never really understood.

What I did understand, though, was that I hated this work with every bone in my body. And every bone in my body felt this hard and harsh work all day and all night. Sometimes I wonder if my pain now is a kind of "memory pain" (like the pain of phantom limbs long gone) of those years in those fields on my knees pulling sacks that weighed more than I did, pulling the end up to hook the wire onto the shiny metal hook and wrapping the strap around the hook off the ground so it could hang free and give a true weight. My bones are still tired because they were violated; my fingers look like I've been picking cotton recently, but I haven't.

I am thankful every single day that I am no longer a field worker, and I am also conscious every day that other people all over the world still are. I cannot go to fancy resorts in the Caribbean, in Mexico, in other exotic locales because I am miserable the entire time I am there, and I make my entire family miserable as well, because I can only see the workers at these places. I watch them walk across the rough fields barefoot to get to work having caught 4:30 A.M. buses so that they can clean our rooms and serve us exotic, sensuous, outrageously expensive (obscene) meals in clothes they carefully packed and put on in the restrooms behind the resort before appearing for us in crisp black and white uniforms, smiles on their faces. I watch them throw all the excess food into locked garbage barrels, forbidden to take any home to their large, hungry families.

I know what it means to be a field worker, and the violence of that work on my body haunts me. I am older than 60; in truth, I feel 160. I have lived so many different lives, and violence has either been front and center in these various phases of my life or stalking at the edges waiting to approach, to strike. I try to keep it at bay, but the memories are vivid; the pain is real.

Violence comes in many forms.

**HEATHER**    I am a breast cancer survivor.

There are the words on the page. Simple to write, not so simple to live.

I am a tenure survivor.

There are the words on the page. Simple to write, not so simple to live.

I have spent my career and my personal life rallying for the improvement of women's health—in the home and in the workplace. I have benefited in countless ways from the centuries of women on whose shoulders I have been lifted.

I am a breast cancer survivor.

A year and a half ago, I was diagnosed with a three-inch cancerous tumor in my left breast. Earlier in the year, I had felt the lump and was pushed through the health care system with the news of a clean ultrasound and a dose of evening primrose oil for my fibrocystic breasts.

I am a tenure survivor.

Seven years ago, with a new baby, Tricia, in my arms, I began my tenure-track journey at a large research institution. I knew I could handle the work of motherhood and professorhood. I had strong instincts, talent, and a lifetime of excellence from two loving parents who were also academics. I also have a loving husband who cleans house, cooks, and thrives on coparenting in addition to his own academic profession.

I am a breast cancer survivor.

The pain in my chest got more serious over the summer, and I knew that it was not "in my head." But I didn't know it was cancer until I had a mammogram and a biopsy and a diagnosis of a tumor so large they would have to "take" my breast. I told them to take both.

I am a tenure survivor.

I have written about my entrée into professor/motherhood before, but the published essay left off shortly after I gave birth to my second daughter, Ellie. That fall, I produced a student-authored stage production and formed the Troubling Violence Performance Project with my colleague, Elaine. That year we scheduled more than thirty performances of the troupe. We also began visiting women who had been imprisoned for killing their abusers. Before we embarked on one of our visits to a prison in northern Missouri, I remember being more nervous about my breasts leaking from not nursing my daughter for a few hours than about entering a high-security prison to interview a woman in for life.

I am a breast cancer survivor.

The story is unique and universal. My body, my family, my friends. Surgery, chemotherapy, radiation.

Slash and burn.

I am a tenure survivor.

My father retired from the academy the same spring Ellie was born. Before her first birthday, he died suddenly from an undiagnosed tumor on his adrenal gland. The picture of health and vibrancy, but he was gone, just gone. I missed the first day of teaching that semester to attend his memorial service.

I am a breast cancer survivor.

No surprise to my colleagues, friends, and family—I wrote a one-woman autobiographical show and called it *Booby Prize: A Comedy about Breast Cancer*. I continue my fight for better women's health and now thrust my own body forth on stage as testimony.

I am a tenure survivor.

I wrote an award-winning play the summer after my dad died. And then I codirected a main stage show of student performance work. After the initial "clean" ultrasound that indicated the tumor was noncancerous, I went to dress rehearsal and told my codirector about my temporary breast cancer scare. We sighed with relief and opened the show.

I am a breast cancer survivor.

For my third-year review toward tenure, my department issued the standard evaluation letter. In it they told me they feared I "had no identity."

I got sick. I was bald. I won awards. I published. I taught my classes. I directed. I performed.

I am a tenure survivor.

It isn't that easy to write either.

But here I am.

ELAINE    Heather keeps reminding me to write the body. So I've just reread what I've written about my body and now I feel humbled, ashamed even. I look over at her, forcing myself to actually look directly at her caved-in chest, the scar where the port was created for them to fill her body with chemotherapy drugs and the beginning of a much larger scar that slashed her body and removed both of her bounteous, full breasts, and I feel diminished by my own selfishness. Yes, my body often hurts. Yes, I have arthritis, and I worked very hard in my youth in the fields. All that is true and real. But my dearest friend, sitting here in the sun across from me, is fighting for her *life*. She believes she got cancer because she was not taking good care of herself. She believes she will die—sooner rather than later. She greets each birthday with trepidation, tentatively, gratefully, not because she does not want to reach the BIG 4-o, the BIG 5-o, the BIGGER 6-o but because she wonders if she will get another blessed birthday with her husband and her two young daughters. "Will this be my last birthday?" "How many more will I get to celebrate?" Death sits on her doorstep in a way I cannot even imagine. I don't really want to admit I am sixty years old. She prays for that many years but seriously doubts she will see sixty years in this lifetime, in this body form. Will they find something new and threatening tomorrow? Next week? Next year? They have already found "suspicious" spots here and there; she's had more radiation and a full hysterectomy.

Heather is six feet tall, a warrior woman striding across campus in a pink tracksuit, laughing loudly, with vibrancy and energy, running fund-raisers for cancer research and performing her award-winning one-woman show, *Booby Prize: A Comedy about Breast Cancer*. Graduate students flock to her door, begging her to take them on, to be their adviser, their mentor, their role model.

She welcomes them in and wonders how long she'll be able to do this. Should she take on anything else? Is it helping her or hurting her? *How does she/how should she take good care of herself?* She asks me. We talk about it. Learn to say no; don't be too quick to take on new students, projects, assignments, courses; but live vibrantly, too. Embrace every day. Go to yoga. Find a therapist. Keep moving. That's what we've decided—keep moving. But this cancer, this violence against her body, is a stalker. There's no doubt about that. It watches her every move; it waits for her in the morning and watches her fall asleep every night. It has entered her bones, her blood, her body, her brain. How do you fight violence that has invaded your very being? How do you fight violence at all, in any form? We keep writing because that's the only thing we can manage to do to keep the questions at bay.

Sitting here with Heather at the lake, I can hear the waterfall near the deck where we sit and write, and I think of blood tumbling over the rocks. I talked about my divorce today with Heather, and it was *not* comfortable for me. She talked about having cancer, and that was not comfortable for either of us.

We just got pedicures, which is in itself something astounding for me to think about. My old feet, the same ones that once traveled down rows of cotton holding steady my once young body straining against the strap of the cotton sack and the weight that snaked down the path between the rows. To sit and have these feet pampered only costs money, and today I can afford such luxury. Right now, in this moment, I sit in cool air writing with water nearby and a dear friend and companion who teaches me how to relax and live, just live and be grateful for every moment. A face-to-face meeting with mortality will do that for you.

At this moment my legs do not hurt, my knees do not hurt. Kathleen, my yoga teacher, instructs us how to do a relaxed body scan. Of course, nothing hurts when I lie still and just breathe. Ah, there is a lesson there, but how to bring that into life is the key to moving the body through the day.

HEATHER *paces back and forth across the stage, reaching for the* *audience. She appears to be pulled in each direction, faster and faster.* *The audience's heads begin to follow her in a rhythm, back and forth,* *back and forth, as if watching a tennis match laid before them.* ELAINE *puts two seats together to make a lounge chair for* HEATHER, *who* *finally collapses on it, stretching out her long legs and spreading her arms* *out to the side.* ELAINE *hands her a glass of water, which she drinks in* *one gulp before beginning to speak to the audience.*

HEATHER   I am spent.

It is the end of October 2007, and I am spent.

October has been declared Domestic Violence Awareness Month in the United States.

Ever since Elaine and I began the troupe, we have had far more invitations to speak to organizations and classes during the month of October than at any other time during the year. In 2004, we performed at least two or three times a week during October.

A year later, when I was diagnosed with breast cancer, the troupe performed twice without me that month. I couldn't perform about domestic violence because I was undergoing a different kind of mutilation of my body to ward off cancer.

October is also Breast Cancer Awareness Month in the United States. There are massive movements to wear pink and celebrate survivorship as well as to mourn those who have been lost to the disease. Since I began performing my one-woman show about my cancer diagnosis, treatment, and recovery, October has been the most popular month for requests for *Booby Prize: A Comedy about Breast Cancer.*

One out of every four women in the United States will experience violence at the hands of an abuser.

One out of every seven women in the United States will be diagnosed with breast cancer.

I have spent my October running from one performance to the other, buying into others' desire for my work in this month, this precious month, this artificially created thirty-one days during which we can talk about how to heal our abused bodies.

We deserve all twelve months of the calendar year for awareness, advocacy, education, and research. Nothing less will suffice.

# Violence at Home

ELAINE  At our house, as the only girl, I knew that certainly did not translate into "special." It meant there was no way I could get my license when I turned sixteen. It meant there was no way I could go cruising in cars with my friends. It meant there was no way I could date boys before my eighteenth birthday. I couldn't wear shorts or go to dances. If I did, my father was convinced I would be "married and ruint" before I turned sixteen. Even with all the rules and with him watching me like a hawk, my father totally expected me to get pregnant and drop out of school. The one place I could shine and get noticed was at school. I loved school; I loved to write; I got good grades. My teachers quietly encouraged me. When I graduated from high school with top honors, no one at school was surprised, but my parents were not at all interested in educating a girl. I met with resistance on every side as I began to talk about why I wanted to attend the teachers college only twenty-five miles away. Since then, I have often heard my mother tell stories about this period in our lives. Her stories tell of *my father's* resistance to my college education and of her support behind the scenes, helping me fight his angry, stubborn immobile stance. *I* think I got to college on my own. The way she tells it, it was only through her persistence and support that I finally moved my belongings into the all-girls' dormitory in the fall of 1965. I don't contradict her, but I know she's remembering it all wrong. She was not supportive, that much I know. I wouldn't get that wrong, would I?

Is it any surprise that before I was twenty, still in college, I married a young, suntanned farmer's son who looked into my eyes with deep intensity before he left for graduate school and then proposed by mail? He was the smartest person I had ever met, and he had noticed *me*. He had never had a girlfriend. He wrote from graduate school that it was time, he felt, for him to marry, that having a stable home life while in graduate school would be a solid base from which to launch his career in biology. He sent in this letter a collage he had crafted from magazines, a pastiche of color and images. The part I remember the most vividly was an odd image of a bride with her head cut off. I did not notice the omen then. He asked whether I would consider marrying him and moving to Illinois. I should let him know by return mail. I didn't even hesitate. It took me about thirty seconds to weigh this proposal against the prospects of marrying the good Baptist boy who groped for my blouse in the dark on our way to church functions. It took a little longer to wonder if my growing relationship with the quiet poet in my English class might blossom. But I knew my parents would never approve of the poet and would push the religious boy. But what would they think of this German Lutheran farmer's son? It just might work. Up to now, I had been an absolutely perfect daughter. Only my brothers had rebellion in their blood. I was terrified to speak my mind to my father; I never questioned anything out loud at home. I had only argued once—to go to college. So I thought this boy might fit the bill. He would take good care of me, and I knew he was my ticket out of Missouri's redneck, conservative boot heel and into a world of books and graduate school, a world that was as alien to me as the stars or a black hole. So I sent back a meek, grateful "Yes."

We married before my twentieth birthday, and I moved to Illinois. Within nine months, I was not pregnant; I did not give birth to a child until several years later. But I did wind up nursing a bleeding ulcer. I had no idea who this stranger was that I had married. He was a cruel and hard man, unflinching in his criticism of everyone in the world, especially me. He sneered at my ineptitudes, took on an air of superiority that crushed my opinions, my hopes, my dreams. He had made a mistake, he thought. I really wasn't as bright as he had calculated. That frustrated him. He didn't make mistakes. I disappeared into myself. I spoke rarely and carefully, never to reveal my inadequacies, my lack of knowledge. I read vociferously. I could eventually talk about quantum physics, bioethics, and the metabolism of the African frogs and toads he used in his laboratory experiments.

I knew microbiology and electronmicroscopy like the back of my hand. I typed his dissertation every night until the red sun came up over the tops of the buildings and lit up the keyboard, my fingers still black and greasy with the smelly liver I fed to his lab frogs. And my stomach bled as I held myself tightly so that I would not explode. One typo, I knew, and he might turn over a lab table and smash the test tubes near my head. He might push me up against the door in the deserted building in the silence of the early morning and tell me again, just for good measure, how lucky I was to be married to him. By virtue of being his wife, he said, I would share in the glory of his brilliance. The world just might notice me, he jeered, if they knew I was his. And I knew that I, too, had made a grave and dangerous mistake. How would I ever escape? I had not a clue.

Without his blessing, I began to apply to graduate programs. Eventually, I got into the Folklore Institute at Indiana University. He came with me. I wasn't really happy to have him there, and one day, very quietly, I began to drive around town looking for a place to hide. Eventually, my graduate school friends, all women, cleared out a closet for me to sleep in.

Recently, I read about a woman who had been killed in Tennessee by her ex-husband. He'd walked into the place where she worked and shot her four times, shot three people sitting close to her in the building, and killed two policemen on the way out the door. I cannot recall now if he killed himself or if he was shot. But I could not get that woman and that man out of my mind. She had taken out several orders of protection against her husband. I had totally forgotten that I had also gone to court once and petitioned for an order of protection. Before that, I'd never even heard of an ex parte or an order of protection.

Lucky for me, my lawyer was a hard, no-nonsense kind of woman who had no use whatsoever for John and all the men like him. She suffered through my bouts of doubts and my confusion and my fear with a sober face and suggested I get everything I could out of this lowlife, as she would call him. Well, I knew John was no low-life; indeed, he was a summa cum laude, brilliant researcher. I knew he was superior to all of us, but I learned not to say that in front of my lawyer. She urged me to let the sheriff take me out to the house where John still lived and get half the furniture, a few of our records, a few photographs. But I would not hear of it. I had taken what I wanted and needed, I declared, not willing to tell her that I simply could not go back to that house, sheriff or no sheriff. We eventually agreed on joint custody of our son. I was not in a bargaining position. Little did I know that because I had left my son out there in the house with my husband and moved into the little yellow house on the corner full of women students, the court would accuse me of child abandonment. What did they know? I had moved my clothes and books into a walk-in closet in the little yellow house because there were no rooms left for one more stranded female, keen to leave a bad situation. I was grateful for the closet and slept on a pad on the floor, listening to my own breath on the dark, hot nights, expecting the worst, expecting him to burst in in the middle of the night and drag me out by my hair—or worse, to burn the whole place down.

I had, he said, embarrassed him. "No one," he would shout, "no one" in his family had ever been divorced. Ever. He told me that a lot. What would he tell his fellow researchers, his adviser at the lab? "Besides," he claimed smugly, "you won't get to the end of next week without me. How will you get around? Who will take care of you? You'll be back."

But I didn't go back. And I did just fine. I rode my bike. In fact, the first morning that I rode that bike from the little yellow house on the corner, across the railroad tracks, and onto the university campus with my books in my backpack, I soared. Never, before or since, had I ever experienced the release of that amazing ride under the summer blue sky. I thought my heart would burst, it felt that good. My stomach slowly began to relax.

It got pretty rocky again, of course. Joint custody meant that we alternated picking up our son from his school on Fridays, but John would get busy in his lab and forget to go get his son. I often got a phone call from the school asking if I could please come pick up my son because he was the last child left there and the teachers needed to go home. One day I came home late from the library, studying for my comprehensive exams. I opened the screen door onto the porch of the farmhouse I was renting and heard a murmur in the corner, under a rickety shelf in the back corner. There, my son sat, hunched over his knees, whimpering like a lost puppy. John had forgotten to pick him up again, so my son decided to walk home. I gasped to think of this tiny first-grader walking along the curvy roads between my house and the school. But I was even more terrified when he explained that he didn't have to walk the whole way because this really nice man picked him up and left him at the door. My heart stopped beating. Had I really lucked out? Had this man picked up my son and driven him courteously to my house and not molested him, not harmed a hair on his little head? My skin crawled with the pure terror, the fear of my little boy's story.

I went back to court to change the custody arrangement. John could not be trusted, I claimed, to pick up his son on alternating Fridays. I told the story of last Friday's events and pleaded for the right to keep my son with me at all times. His father could come to my house and pick him up. He could stay in his lab until midnight and I would not care, as long as I knew exactly where my son was and that he was safe. John didn't show up at the courthouse and protest my efforts, but he showed up at my house that same afternoon, madder than hell. He seethed. He raged. He called me names. How dare I? What gave me the right to slander his name in front of a judge and other people? How dare I? I felt myself backing out of the living room where he stood shaking his finger at my face, backing into the kitchen, away from the counter where the knives were. He followed me, a dark moving cloud of fury. He picked up a glass and threw it; it whizzed past my ear and made a hole in the wall behind my head. I did not know if his aim was off. I doubted it. Had he wanted to hit me with the glass, I'm certain he could have. I knew I was in grave danger. I had dared to defy him. I had left him. I had tried to take away his son. He reminded me then of my father, a man suffering from posttraumatic syndrome after World War II (long before they had a name for it)—a boiling mass of pure anger with nowhere to put it, no way to release it. I'd seen this before, and I knew to get out of the way because I had watched my mom avoid my father's rages, his bitterness, his criticism, his fists. Our son walked in and the fury dissipated ever so slightly. John backed off, taking his son with him out my front door.

After I stopped shaking, I called my lawyer. Months later, at the divorce hearing, I wore the only suit I owned, a thick, wool tweed that I wore like armor. My girlfriends were dressed to go with me in their summer dresses, skirts, and sleeveless tops. They worried that I might pass out in the August heat in Indiana, but I was determined to wear that suit. It was the only protection I had that day.

Being a girl with three brothers did not make me feel special in my father's house. Rather, I was "protected," because my reputation seemed to be everybody's business, even my rowdy brothers' concern. I always felt I had something to prove—that I wasn't a slut and I wasn't going to get pregnant and "have" to get married, and mostly that I wasn't smart enough to send to college, especially because my brothers weren't at all interested in that. But I did go to college; eventually, I even went to graduate school, but only after I had found a way to escape from the violence in my home. And my relationship with my family, my birth family, is strained. I remember getting asked to leave the house because I disagreed with some racial slurs my brothers insisted on using at the dinner table when we were all adults. My father was shocked that I was angry and was actually standing up for the "niggers," as he so bluntly put it. So certain topics are definitely off-limits—well, most topics are still off-limits in my family. So the talk is cheerful, surface chatter that feels fake to me. I'm never myself there. How can I be? I'm a professor at the largest research institution in the state; I've written books; I have Ph.D. students. Most of this simply doesn't compute to them. So I just make my pumpkin pies for Thanksgiving and try to stay only one night before heading back to my own home. My kids love it at Grandma's; they love the big family gatherings, the food, the smells, the banter, the laughter. I don't tell them the backstory—why would I do that? Everyone needs an extended family. My son was great friends with my one niece until she died. Actually, that's a story that belongs in this book. Her younger sister, Missy, was ten when Cynthia died. Missy might tell the story this way:

"My Dead Sister's Sad Story"
I used to have a sister. Her name was Cynthia. I miss her a lot, but some days I can't remember exactly what her face looked like. But I can always look at all the pictures of her around the house when that happens. I do know Cyn was a really pretty girl; everybody says that. Not just cute like me, but really pretty, a tiny girl with rich, bouncy reddish brown hair falling naturally down her back in shiny curls. "Hair to die for" was how everyone at church would put it. That's what I remember most from all the photos, too, both before and after—that amazing hair. It was naturally red, but with all that blood it looked alive, even when it wasn't. Not like mine, so straight I can't do a thing with it.

Cyn graduated from high school. I remember that day and remember just how proud the whole family was when she told us she was going to college, to enroll in the nursing school. It just might be true that of all our immediate family, only Cynthia and me went to college—except, of course, we knew Aunt Elaine had gone to college, too. Dad was so pleased that he bought Cynthia a little red car, and every day he would get up real early with her and she would drive about thirty miles to the city to go to school—exactly the same school where Aunt Elaine had gone, in fact. Grandpa didn't think it would last. He said she'd be pregnant and "ruint" within the year, but Cyn just ignored him and smiled really pretty like we all did when Grandpa was carping. He said that about all us girls; Aunt Elaine said he used to say it about her, too. Might have been because Grandma was maybe already knocked up when she married Grandpa. Nobody has ever suggested that, but I recently did the math. She was about fifteen and he was sixteen, but then he lied about his age and went off to war, leaving her with a tiny baby. Of course, Cyn did have a boyfriend who wasn't going to college. She knew that might be a problem, but she just kept saying she wanted to be a nurse.

I've heard everyone in my family tell the story of "that night." Aunt Elaine always tells about the "dreaded" phone call that came around three o'clock in the morning. You always know that a call at that time of night is one of two things: either really, really bad news or a wrong number. She says she picked up the phone praying it was a wrong number. It wasn't.

Grandpa called her and all the other family members. By the time he called Aunt Elaine, she could hardly hear his voice as he tried to speak through his sobs. "It's Cynthia. It's Cynthia. Someone shot our Cynthia, and she's gone. She's dead." Aunt Elaine got to our house in under three hours; she must have driven ninety miles an hour in the dark to get here.

I really didn't wake up until around six o'clock in the morning, and by then our house was buzzing with people, the smell of coffee, the phone ringing off the hook. I peeked out my window and was terrified to see the sheriff's car with the red lights still going round and round in the near dark sitting in our driveway. He was getting out of the car with my dad and Grandpa. I learned they had just come back from the "scene of the crime." The rest of the next twenty-four hours are kind of a blur. I crept out of the room and ran smack into my little brother, who was crouched in the hall, just as scared as me. We found parents and grandparents, aunts and uncles, at the kitchen table, staring at the wood surface with blank faces. My mom was just staring, not saying anything. She didn't even look at us.

I don't know how, but I can still see that scene just down the road from our country house with amazing detail in my mind, even though I was never there when it was a "crime scene." I guess it's because I heard that story so many times over the next few days, weeks, even months, now years. And some days they would let me sit in on the trial even though I was barely ten. That's where I saw the huge blown-up pictures of Cynthia slumped over in her car, nothing but wild red hair and blood. Her face was nearly erased, but there was no mistaking that amazing hair. That's when Aunt Elaine took me for a long walk around the small town. I knew it was to get me out of seeing more of those pictures.

The story I pieced together was that at about 2:00 A.M., a man going home late had driven up the ramp at the interstate exit and found a small red car with its lights on, motor still running, and a woman dead inside covered in blood from gunshot wounds. According to this story, this man called the sheriff's office, and eventually the sheriff and my dad and my grandfather went to the scene, a place on the overpass that is almost visible from our house—it's that close. Of course, we had all been sleeping soundly as Cyn died on that interstate ramp in the dark, something my dad has never forgotten or forgiven himself for. These are the facts as I heard them at the trial: Cynthia had been on her way home from town, a rowdy place just south of where we live. She had been to see her boyfriend at his mother's house and then had briefly gone to a party. She was driving home when someone she apparently knew approached her car. Here's where it gets fuzzy in the telling. She was sitting in the driver's seat when she was found, as I just said, with the lights still on, the motor running, the driver's side window rolled down. But they discovered she was barefoot, and they found one of her shoes at the bottom of the embankment and mud and grass stains on her bare feet. Why had she gotten out of the car? Had she been forced out of the car, been attacked or raped, and then somehow gotten back into the driver's seat before being shot three times in the head at close range? We never got good answers to all these questions, or at least they never told me. That's what makes it all so spooky.

Her boyfriend was questioned, of course, like a hundred times, as were many of the people they both knew and the people who had been at the party. But the guy they prosecuted, who is still in jail, was just a kid from across the river. He was

nineteen, exactly Cyn's age. People said this guy showed up at
a lot of local parties, but everyone knew he wasn't from around
here. No one really knew him, but he kind of developed a
thing for Cynthia. He'd go to parties where he thought she'd
show up. But her friends said she didn't really like him and
wouldn't go driving with him. He was kind of greasy, a kind of
tough guy, fancied himself as a ladies' man, wore a black leather
jacket but drove a kind of junky car. At the trial, folks began to
remember how he would bug her, ask her out, even follow her
when she left parties. The prosecutor argued that on the night
"in question," this guy followed Cyn all the way to the highway
ramp, that one right near our own house. Somehow, he got her
to stop and roll down her window. They argued; he kept begging
her to give him a chance, to go out with him. The script here
is, of course, invisible. We really don't know what happened on
that ramp in the dark. But she had stopped the car, the window
was rolled down, the motor was still running, and she was most
definitely dead with three bullets in her head.

Actually, as I think about it, no one told me if she had been
raped. But really, I was just a kid then, and during the days I
was allowed to go to the trial, no one talked about that. Maybe
they figured a rape didn't really matter if the woman was found
already dead. I wondered if my dad asked the prosecutor to
keep that part out of the record just to save face for Cyn. It was
all kind of like a dream. They really, really tried to make Cyn
look like a bad girl. There were questions about what she was
wearing, did she usually drive with her shoes off (like that was
a big no-no, a sin even), did she do drugs, did she hang with the
wrong crowd. I thought they were trying to say she was a slut.
Of course these were ridiculous questions if you knew Cynthia.
She was just such a good girl; it made me sick or want to laugh.
Did they really think she would even think about breaking the
law or breaking God's laws? We went to church three or four
times a week. She was a perfect Christian girl; even Grandpa
says that now—"the perfect little girl."

Well, that guy's in prison. I sat there at the trial and watched his face. I would just stare at him up there all spruced up, no leather jacket, no long hair now. He never said a word. Not one word. I hope he did it, because if he didn't, well, you know, his life's over, too. He got sixty years, but they say he might get out of prison in less than twenty years. That makes me a little scared, actually.

At Cynthia's funeral, we sang "When We All Get to Heaven," and the preacher told us that God works in mysterious ways. He told us that we don't always know or can't understand God's plan for our lives. He told us to believe that it was just Cynthia's time to go. He told us that God just wanted her in heaven because he loved her so much. I never said a word. Not one word. And neither did Aunt Elaine.

ELAINE   Lately I've been thinking I would like to get the transcripts of Cynthia's murder trial. Like Missy, I have only blurred memories now of that time. Where I grew up, folks didn't even lock the doors to their homes or their cars. This kind of violence just didn't happen in our community, to our family. But it did. And it made us afraid. Now they lock their doors, and there's always a fresh wreath on that ramp off the interstate where they found Cynthia's little red car. I'm not even sure who keeps replacing it, but every time I go back there, there it is, reminding me. And I always look at that spot and down the embankment and wonder what actually happened that night almost within hearing distance of Cynthia's house, where the windows were open and the doors unlocked.

And it does not seem to stop, this violence nearby, in our families, affecting those we love and cherish. I got a phone call last week from one of my dearest friends. She's eighty-seven and doing really well. She never misses the women's basketball games, and we're both in a small book club where we read the likes of Carolyn Heilbrun, Barbara Kingsolver, and Annie Lamont. I first met her when I was doing field research for my books on clergywomen. She was a minister for nearly fifty years before she retired, but she still occasionally gives a sermon or does a weddings for a friend or family member. She is one of my role models for how to age gracefully, with vibrancy and energy. But when she called, she was weeping uncontrollably; I simply could not understand what she was trying to tell me.

Finally I realized she was saying her granddaughter—her brilliant, musical, beautiful, talented granddaughter—had been shot in the head by her boyfriend in front of some of their mutual friends. She had recently broken up with him, my friend said between deep, wrenching sobs, so he waited for her at a favorite restaurant, approached her and her friends, and shot her in the parking lot. Then he turned the gun on himself and blew his brains out over the front of the car. "Why?" my friend kept asking me. "Why does this happen? Whatever could have caused him to react with this kind of deadly violence?" They are both gone now, and their friends will carry this scene in their minds for the rest of their lives. All of us will. "Elaine," she told me, "you must write about this—more. You must write more about this."

Helpless, I finally put down the phone and wept because I simply do not know how to write "more about this." Some of this feels new—young men killing their girlfriends—intimate violence beginning in high school and college. I keep hearing stories from my clergywomen friends, from colleagues, from acquaintances, from the shelter director. It no longer suffices to talk about "domestic violence," because this violence in our midst is insidious and is occurring in the halls of our high schools, even junior high, when boys become excessively jealous, directing their girlfriends about whom they can hang out with, have lunch with, drive in cars with, be friends with, calling or texting them hundreds of times a day, checking on where they are and who they are with.

This possessiveness, this male entitlement begins very early. And when it is thwarted, when the boys don't get their way, when the girls rebel and move away, the boys sometimes react violently. They use their fists; they stalk; they are persistent with threats online and with the telephone; and some of them kill. We should be worried. We should be very worried.

ELAINE *turns to write in her notebook, while* HEATHER *reads aloud from hers.*

HEATHER   I have just finished tucking my four-year-old into bed. She usually drifts to sleep while I sing her a lullaby. My seven-year-old is reading a Nancy Drew book in an overstuffed chair in the loft. I kiss them both on the forehead and head downstairs to see Bill. He offers to rub my feet, and we begin to relax into our evening. We drift in and out of conversation, watching a news show on TV. There is a story about a teenage girl who was stalked and abused by her high school boyfriend. Outraged, we can't watch. Bill turns it off and says he just doesn't know what he would do if anyone hurt his daughters. I nod in agreement. He mentions the creepy guy who used to follow me around in high school. I remember it well. Cole started out nice enough, but then he wouldn't take "Go away" for an answer. Even when geography separated us for college, he showed up on my dorm room doorstep, uninvited and unwelcome.

Years after we dated, I saw him in a restaurant; my first impulse was to dive under the table where we were eating. Bill peered down under the booth and asked me if I was OK. I nodded my head and then explained who had walked past. I just didn't know what to say, what to do, or how to acknowledge Cole without causing him to begin contacting me again. And even though girlhood was long behind me, I still wasn't going there.

I do not want my daughters to question themselves if an abuser enters their life. I want them to know how to say "No" and how to say "Go." I want them to know that controlling behaviors can start small, like having a boy- or girlfriend want to know where you are at all times. Red flags should not just go up but should wave fervently—This is a controlling person! Do not be fooled by his (or her) controlling ways!

Because I grew up in an unabusive household, my instincts told me that Cole's manner wasn't right, and when he told me that no one would ever love me the way he loved me, I knew to say good-bye. But the girl on TV didn't get that chance. Stalking stories, you see, usually end quite similar to the ones on that report—the girl is found beaten, molested, and dead.

ELAINE   Alice Walker reminds us to go in search of our mothers' gardens to find evidence of the beauty they created in their otherwise barren lives; Virginia Woolf says we tell our own stories backward through our mothers' and our grandmothers' stories. When we do this kind of remembering work to bring our mothers' stories into the present, there is a sense of joy and nostalgia for the recognition of lives we perhaps never really knew. But this work also has another side, a darker side that reminds us that we are indeed our mothers' daughters. And for many of our mothers, their gardens were not enough to heal their wounds or enable them to be strong enough to help us when we most need them. I was not prepared to discover in the stories from battered women a persistent story of disconnection from their mothers. Their stories eventually led me to uncover some of the truth of my mother's story and eventually link it back to the women's stories in this research. I believe the link is an important part of this work. Daughters all, we know the pain of abandonment from mothers who could bear no more pain.

Some time ago, about two years now, I asked my mother if I could tape-record her life story. I had finished research on the life stories of women ministers and had emerged on a project collecting the stories of battered women. I was still high on the potential for these stories to tell us about each other and about ourselves. I wrote my mother a long letter outlining the usefulness of these stories and how much I could learn about her from doing it, even appealing to her need to see me more often to talk her into a polite, even interested "Yes." What I received was an emphatic, resounding, "No."

I was insulted, flabbergasted, and confused. How could she say no to me, the dutiful daughter, the researcher, the writer? But she did. She claimed that right with more power and authority than perhaps I had ever encountered from her. When I finished being angry, I was even more astonished that she had mustered up the courage to make this statement about her right to the privacy of her own life.

Her answer? She said too many people were still alive; there were too many people who might possibly get hurt or misunderstand if she did this, knowing I meant to use the story somehow in a publication not yet imagined. "You tell *your* story," she told me in the voice I had come to hate over the years, "and in doing that you can also tell what you know about mine. But it will still be your story, not mine, and you have every right to do that, you know." At the time, I had no intention of ever telling my story, and I felt I knew only fragments of hers—not nearly enough. So, I put the idea completely away, thinking the episode was over.

But as I began to work more and more with the stories from the women in the shelter and spent tedious hours transcribing the tapes of the women who had agreed to tell me their life stories and the stories of abuse they had endured, my mother's story and her mother's story began to haunt me, as did my own. I heard their stories and my own in the stories of the women on the tapes; I heard my words in theirs; their stories, my mother's stories, and my stories sometimes swirled together in my mind as I walked on the trail near my house, trying to sift through all the transcriptions. In the air in front of my eyes, I actually watched my mother's and grandmother's stories and my own weave in and out of the ones I had collected and listened to over and over and over again on tape.

I came to realize in a visceral, nauseating moment that our mothers have been too wounded themselves to give to us a sense of our own value and worth. I have come to realize that their pain and sadness were so overwhelming they simply did not possess the energy to actually see us and provide for us a safe haven where we could be nurtured to grow in positive ways. So we sought that empowerment, attention, and worth elsewhere. But because we had no sense of our own humanness and value going into relationships beyond our home of origin, we were ill equipped to seek better situations.

This is a part of the cycle of abuse that has never before been included: our mothers and grandmothers have perpetuated a sad tradition of neglect and pain passed through generations of abuse. They, too, left their mothers in a vague, dizzy moment of aloneness and woke the next morning to find themselves locked into newly abusive marriages that sapped their energies and left them vacant and pained. This legacy they passed on to their daughters, not by plan or intent but just by who they were and what they were not able to give. In fact, I think their stories lay bare what lies at the very heart of how women come to find themselves in abusive relationships and why women cannot extricate themselves from the partners who hate and hit them.

Oddly enough, even though I have been immersed in an ethnographic study of a battered women's shelter and have written a book about women's narratives of abuse and violence, I only recently connected the dots about my life. By meeting a first cousin, basically for the first time, I found a link in my own encounters with domestic violence. My cousin grew up in a loving family and spent her summers playing at our grandmother's house and at her paternal grandmother's house. She told me how the rest of the family worried about my mother and the isolation her husband had imposed on our small family, keeping them from visiting, never encouraging visits, connections, reunions. I have recently been able to write some about the violence my father imposed on those of us who lived in his house—about how he "unmade our world," as Elaine Scarry (1985, 19–21) put it—I have fit my own household into the larger picture of violence and abuse that I was trying to study and write about. The work I am doing has helped me realize just how difficult this work is for other women. I'm the scholar. I'm supposed to know what I'm seeing under the microscope. How could I have missed it? It was right under my nose.*

---

* A slightly different version of Elaine's story here also appears in de Caro 2008.

# Curtain Call

*The women rise as the sounds and lights of the lake fade away. They pack up the items from the umbrella table.* HEATHER *removes her sun hat and protective clothing.*

*Lights fade. When they come back up, the two women are at a round kitchen table with laptops and manuscript pages, cell phones, pens, etc.*

ELAINE By ten o'clock the morning after we returned from our writing retreat, Heather was already calling me.

HEATHER (*laughing*) "Do you miss me yet? Are you writing?"

ELAINE That was the message she left on the cell phone I couldn't find.

Writing already. I had barely dragged myself out of bed five minutes before the phone rang, and I was already a bit out of sorts helping my youngest daughter locate the navy blue softball socks she needed for today's games at twelve, three, and six o'clock.

"They were right here!" she bellowed, impatient and put out. "We need some laundry rules in this house." She stormed out of the room heading for another place to look.

Hmmm, I thought, what a novel idea—household rules about clothes, shoes, laundry. I'd never been much for rules. I was more of a consensus kind of girl myself, but maybe that's not the best way to raise kids or run a household. Certainly, I always requested that everyone do his or her own laundry, pick up his or her own shoes, take his or her clothes out of the dryer, and not throw other people's laundry into a basket to wrinkle. I had to laugh out loud as I counted seven—yes, seven!—pairs of my daughter's shoes on the mudroom floor. I gently reminded her, "Well, we do have some rules—like, for example, putting shoes on the white shelves provided."

"Rules," she glared, truly mystified. "Those are rules? I know you want us to pick them up and you tell me to please pick them up sometimes, but I didn't know that was a rule." She slammed the door as she headed for the softball field in her black socks, afraid the coach would not let her play if she showed up in the wrong color. Relieved, I made coffee, knowing I had forty-five whole minutes before I needed to head out to the fields.

I had been gone only two and a half days, yet already I was at fault. She was irritated; things weren't in the right place. They were out of kilter. Suddenly, the spa and the waterfalls seemed far more than a few miles away.

I grabbed my coffee and went outside to sit in the sun, listen to the birds, and drink my coffee alone.

When, I wondered, had Heather found time to write or to call me as she woke up to the chattering demands of her two young girls, needy because she, too, had been away?

But Heather's message also said she had been thinking about the book. And that, I thought, was easier—and, indeed, I too had been thinking about the book. How could I not? We had basically eaten, drunk, and lived this book for the days we had left behind the messiness of our lives. And that had been the idea—the devoted, dedicated, uninterrupted time had laid the groundwork for this return to "real" life. The challenge was to allow the writing to continue, to invite it into the messiness and find ways to nourish and nurture it, even as we looked for escaped socks, attended to children, and fed animals. Last night, out of habit, I turned on my e-mail for exactly ten seconds before I realized that I could not—no, I would not—read it until at least Monday or Tuesday of next week. Some messiness is beloved and necessary. Other unwanted intrusions can be ignored with gleeful abandon.

I picked up my pen and wrote this down before I forgot and before I went to bake in the sunshine at my daughter's softball games.

*HEATHER rises from her chair and addresses the audience.*

**HEATHER**  The day after Christmas this past year, Elaine got a telephone call at her home from a local judge. He presides over the court sessions in which "petitioners" come to seek ex partes and orders of protection against "respondents" they are afraid of. We know this judge; he's an elected official, and we had heard stories about him—not negative, just suggestive. He called Elaine because he has read her book, and he wants to talk to her about some of the things she writes in chapter 3 about how hard it is for women to articulate, to actually speak, the violence they have endured. But, he explained to her at length, it's impossible for a judge, for someone like him, to pass any kind of judgment if the victim cannot, does not, speak the violence. He says he wants to say to her, "Get the marbles out of your mouth, Woman, and tell me exactly what this man has done; tell me so I can help you." But, he says, more often the woman cannot speak the violence, leaving him to make a decision without any real evidence. Elaine asks whether a woman's word is clear evidence that a man has been abusive. "Well," he replies, "it's something. At least it's something."

Elaine wants to know what the abuser says. What does "he" say, she asks the judge? What does a batterer say in defense of his actions? What does he say about her? About himself? "Interesting question," the judge responds. "Why don't you come sit in and hear for yourself?" Elaine and I think this is a great idea.

# A Courtroom Scene

**ELAINE** For weeks I sat in on the court sessions every day. Judge Marshall is there to grant or not grant protection to women whose body language assaults me as I am sitting alone, listening, a covert subject, trying to hear the "he said/she said" firsthand. I am not prepared for these scenes. Even working at the shelter, I was removed from the immediacy of this confrontational setting; it feels obscene, the private loosed in a public space for all to see and hear. I feel embarrassed for them. I can feel how thin my own skin is here. I feel vulnerable. I think I know how she feels.

They both have lawyers. The judge asks her to take the stand. When she moves from the safe place behind a large table near her lawyer, she must walk in front of the "respondent," her abusive, violent, angry, ex-husband. Her new husband sits behind me and to the left, a soft, large man, obviously uncomfortable having to be here, to hear this conversation about the man his wife used to sleep with, cook for, with whom she shares a son. She looks neither right nor left, but she holds her right hand on her swollen belly, pregnant now with another man's child. I can tell she would love to run out the back door, but she walks resolutely to the chair and makes certain she is turned more toward the judge than toward her ex, who is now about ten feet away from her. He sits so still; I wonder if he's stopped breathing. He is about the same distance from me, but all I can see is the back of his shaved head, the bulging muscles under his Carhartt coat, his stained jeans. When she sits, the woman visibly curls her body as though to protect herself and her belly. She is poised for flight, a pretzel in a bulging pink sweater.

The judge asks her if she is still afraid of this man, indicating the respondent. She murmurs a faint "Yes." The judge tells her she'll have to speak up so he and the court recorder can hear her. It is very important, he says, for her to be clear and to speak up. OK? OK.

"Now, state your name for the record, and tell me if this man has threatened you recently. I see here this is your third time to come to this court asking for orders of protection. You want another full year's protection, is that correct?" (I try to remember every word of this scene for what follows is not a transcript.)

"Yes."

"And?"

"I am still afraid of him."

"Has he threatened you?"

"No. Not really."

"Not really. What do you mean by not really?"

"Well, my son told me he has a weapon in his truck."

"Do you know for a fact that he has a weapon in his truck?"

"No, only that my son said he saw it."

"Why would your son tell you that? Did your son say that your ex-husband was threatening to hurt someone, to hurt you, with the weapon?"

"No. No, he did not."

"So what makes you think he's going to hurt you with it?"

"I just believe he's still angry."

"And what does he do when he's angry?"

"He has, in the past, hurt me, thrown things."

"How has he hurt you?"

"He—he used to hurt me a lot."

"OK. I see we're not going anywhere with this. Can you tell me if he has hurt you in the past three years?"

"No."

"Has he threatened you in the past three years?"

"No. But I brought this letter he sent me after I got remarried. I can tell he's still really angry. The stuff he says."

"Do we have the letter here? OK. Let me see the letter. [pause] Why do you think he's still feeling the way he was when he wrote this letter?"

"I just know him. I know what he's like. And now I'm married and I'm pregnant. And I'm still afraid of him. About three weeks ago, he called my house and ordered our son to get me on the phone to talk to him. I don't know what he was angry about, but I could hear him yelling in the phone halfway across the room. But I refused to go to the phone. But him asking to talk to me, wasn't that a violation of the order of protection? He's not supposed to talk to me, right? But he was screaming for our son to put me on the phone so he could yell at me."

"Did you go to the phone and talk to him?"

"No, sir."

"OK. That's how an order of protection works, you see. You don't have to talk to him. You are right that he was not supposed to ask to speak to you, but you had the right to refuse to talk to him. Right? And you have that right even if you don't have an order of protection, don't you? Even if you don't have an order of protection, you do not have to talk to him. At all. Ever. Do you understand that? That is your right—not to talk to him."

"Yes, sir."

"OK. That's enough. You go sit down over there and I want to hear from the respondent. Come on up here. State your name for the record and have a seat."

"Now, why do you think this woman is still afraid of you?"

"I have no idea, Judge. I have not spoken to her or even been up close to her in more than two years."

"Do you have a weapon in your car?"

"Yes, I do, for protection."

"Did you on any occasion indicate you had intentions to use that weapon to harm your son's mother?"

"No, sir, I did not."

"Would you verify that you wrote this letter?"

"I did."

"Would you read the third paragraph aloud, please?"

"'I cannot believe you are gone. You were my whole life and you still are. I still cannot imagine any kind of life without you. I cannot imagine another man touching you.'"

"Did you write those words?"

"Yes, sir, I did."

"Do you still hold those feelings for your ex-wife?"

"Yes, sir, I do."

"But would you do anything now to harm her, her new husband, or her unborn child?"

"No, sir, I would not."

"She says you used to hurt her. Is that true?"

"Well, sometimes, when things was rough we'd argue a lot and maybe sometimes I'd drink too much and slap her around a bit, but I never really hurt her. I never meant to really hurt her, ever."

"But you did hurt her?"

"Yes, sir, I did."

"Why would you hurt her?"

"Well, like I said, things was rough sometimes. I didn't have no job, and we had a baby and she wasn't working—I didn't really want her to work. So we didn't have any money and the baby got sick or whatever. And, sometimes, she'd get pissed off that I wasn't bringing home any money and the baby was sick. I don't know. It was just all bad and I felt bad. But I always felt bad when I hurt her, too."

"Well, I don't care what your problems were or are. Having problems or drinking or whatever does not give you the right to hurt her or your son. Do you understand that? It never gives you the right to hurt anyone. Do you get that? Do you clearly understand it is not OK to hurt someone else just because you've got problems?"

"Yes, sir, I know that."

"I get that all the time in here. Things were bad. There's no money. The babies are sick. She's not working or not working hard enough. Or whatever. And lots of times there's drugs and alcohol involved. And I don't care about all of that. Do you hear me? I don't care what's going on. It's not an excuse to hit her or slap her around or hurt her. That's what you need to hear me say, right now. Do you understand?"

"Yes, sir."

"OK. Go sit down. I'm speaking now to the petitioner. I believe this man has hurt you in the past. I also believe he's still pretty angry that you've moved on in your life, found a new husband, and are now pregnant. I also believe he may still feel the things he wrote in that letter you brought in. I know all of this, but I do not feel I have heard any evidence that he has recently threatened you in any way. I have not heard that he threatened to harm you in the presence of your son. Therefore, I do not believe I have enough evidence of any kind that suggests this man is going to try to harm you. If he does, I want you to come right back in here and tell this court what he has done and we will give you an order of protection."

"And, you—I'm speaking now to the respondent. Leave her alone. Whether or not there's an official order of protection in place, you are to leave this woman alone. Do you understand that? And if you wind up back in here with her saying you have bothered her in any way or harmed her in any way, you will not like what I will charge you with in response. Is that clear?"

"Hereby let the record show that I am requiring the respondent to pay the petitioner's court costs for today's session. Case closed."

Then the judge said to me, "I'm glad you could make it. You're the only one left in the room. See what I mean? This is the place to hear it all, to really hear it all. Come on back; I'll give you a cup of coffee. We'll talk."

I see the judge's problem; I know he needs evidence to grant an order of protection. But he knows that guy. He recognizes him. He's seen him a hundred times before. Big, burly, shaved head, tough, mean, spiteful. Or soft-spoken, well dressed, respectful. Order of protection or not, he will hurt that woman. None of us doubted that for a moment.

She knows what he does when he's angry, and he's plenty angry right now. Plenty angry.

Between court visits to observe, I'm reading Michael Kimmel, the father of "masculinity studies." He sounds like a nice enough kind of guy. He says he founded masculinity studies after reading and appreciating feminist studies. It's a feminist model, he says, of understanding the construction of the male in modern society. He's smart and convincing. In a recent interview, he tries to help the listener understand what it is like to be raised male in American culture. This may hold true for other cultures as well, but he doesn't want to generalize. In American culture, he says, the typical white, straight man knows that the whole world thinks he has power, cache, respect, status, authority. Yet according to Kimmel, the individual white, straight man does not feel powerful. Men tell him, "I feel powerless. So, the aggression then is to restore the balance . . . trying to relevel the playing field" (Kimmel n.d.).

Kimmel tries hard to make a case for the beaten-down white, straight man who thinks he should be entitled to power and authority but who as an individual man just trying to make it from day to day does not feel powerful. He is convincing in his understanding of why this man feels let down, cheated, trapped, not given his due. His wife, his kids, his boss do not respect him. He's missed his entitlement to power and authority. He misses feeling powerful, if he ever did. Kimmel dismisses much of the Iron John and Promise Keepers rhetoric, saying that the rhetoric of both "seek the Warrior inside" and "find the nurturing man inside" are missing the mark for most white, straight men. He does not try to justify why these men would hit their wives and kids. He does not do that, but it's right below the surface; I can feel it through my very thin skin.

There's a story I assign in my women's literature course. It was written in the 1940s by an African American writer, Ann Petry. "Like a Winding Sheet" is the story of the marriage of an African American man and woman who light up each other's lives. They find each other in spite of the horrors of urban life, crime, unhappiness, poverty, unemployment, pain, and the times. They are deeply in love and cannot wait until the end of the day, when they can be together—a fairy tale beginning. But the man has it bad when he leaves the small apartment where his lovely wife waits for his sure return. Because he is black, his white female boss picks on him and gives him extra tasks long after he is scheduled to leave; the woman at the corner coffee shop tells him she has no more coffee even though he can see that the pot is steaming and full. All day long he suffers at the hands of rude, racist neighbors and strangers. Day after day he deals with the pain of being black, of being dehumanized, slighted, hurt, disrespected. Although he has never before hit her, one night he comes home late after yet another demoralizing day and beats her until she lies lifeless on the floor. My students never understand the title of that story. I always have to explain to them that the "winding sheet" is what might be wrapped around her dead body when they take her out of the apartment. Not a fairy-tale ending.

Kimmel's interview and his textbooks, his articles, his speeches remind me of this small, fairly unnoticed short story. In fact, the story is told from the point of view of the young black man. We feel his pain; we walk in his shoes; we suffer his indignities; we understand his anger. But like his wife, we are not prepared for his violence.

As the judge said to the respondent in the courtroom. "It does not matter how bad your day was. I don't care what kind of troubles you've got. Do you hear me? That never gives you an excuse to harm her, to hit her. Do you understand? That is never, ever an excuse."

I wonder if Kimmel would agree.

# A Conference Scene

*Obvious lecture situation. Several people are sitting at desks, taking notes, chatting, while the next speaker moves to the podium.* ELAINE *and* HEATHER *are in the audience. The speaker is a striking woman, dressed to the nines, heels, very businesslike. She carries a stack of tan folders, all with black plastic spiral bindings. With some effort, she slaps them down on the table next to the podium.*

CARRIE SMYTHE  Hello, I'm Carrie Smythe. I am the director of the state Coalition against Domestic Violence, which is located in the capital city. We work with the state government, lobbying for battered women's rights, and we oversee all sixty-three state shelters for battered women. I am also a councilwoman for this town. I know most of you know me—very well. *[She laughs a bit as though she knows they think she's a bit of a pain.]* Although I know you are expecting a polished speech up here today during this really critical conference of lawyers, teachers, judges, lawmakers, and shelter workers, I have decided to do something totally different. I am going to tell you about some women—fourteen, to be exact—who are currently in prison serving life sentences with no chance of parole for killing their abusers.

Most of these women were accused of killing their abusers or plotting to kill their abusers, even if they didn't personally pull the trigger. And they were all sentenced before the legal defense of battered women's syndrome came into being. So the fact that they had been battered, beaten, raped, and violated for years by their boyfriends and husbands—that information was not even allowed into the court records when they were prosecuted. It was considered not relevant. So, all of them—yes, hear me out—all of them were sentenced to life in prison with no chance of parole—ever. I have with me here some rather lengthy clemency files that have been created by the law schools in our state in an attempt to get clemency for these women, all of whom are currently incarcerated in state prisons.

These files were delivered to the office of the governor, but as you all know, he died very unexpectedly and apparently never reviewed them. There were high hopes that his successor might sign them during her short tenure in the governor's office, but for some reason, her staff never brought them to her attention. Of course, some members of the state House and Senate have identified these as very important files and have been trying for years to get our new governor to review them and free these women, many of whom have already served more than twenty-five or thirty years in prison. Our own district representative has made this one of her top priorities. But so far to no avail. The governor has not apparently ever even seen the clemency files. But we are not giving up. In fact, what I want to do today is have some kind of impact on this audience. I may be speaking to the choir here, but we really, really need to mobilize around this issue. These are real women, sitting in prison, hoping they will be granted clemency so they can still spend a few years with their families and with their children and grandchildren. I read you their names [reading slowly, dispassionately, clearly]:

Sharon Walker
Alicia Gonzales
Buena Molder
Corinne Vortez
Maggie Black
Jennifer Stewart
Ruth Bailey
Wanda Moore
Rebecca Shoemaker
Madeline Parker
Cathy Nowell
Patricia Kirk
Peggy McDonald
Mary Franklin*

---

* All are pseudonyms.

*The audience is uncomfortable yet entranced as the speaker reads the names on the files, one after another, stacking them on the table beside the podium.*

**CARRIE SMYTHE** Thank you.

*She picks up the stack of files and exits off the stage. Huddled over their laptops, ELAINE and HEATHER write and talk excitedly.*

**HEATHER** I know what we should do next.

**ELAINE** Absolutely! I know the law professor who teaches the third-year rotation for cases of domestic violence. I think we could get copies of those clemency files. They should be public records.

**HEATHER** We should go see them—the women—in prison, talk to them. We should get their stories in their own words. Those clemency files have been written by lawyers; they've rewritten their stories for the courtroom. We need to hear their actual stories, in their own words. We could do what Rhodessa Jones did (Fraden 2000). Maybe we could actually begin a troupe in the women's prison with women telling their own stories and talking about their "life, with no chance of parole" sentences.

**ELAINE** I'm ready when you are.

*Lights fade on the two women as the scene from their new play begins to unfold.*

# Life, with No Chance

*Lights up on a prison scene encircled in a harsh spotlight with bars over it. Two female ethnographers are entering a prison. They come from offstage, loaded with tape recorders, bags, pads of paper, etc. struggling a bit to get to the prison's front door. They stand a bit confused, reading the directions about pressing the buzzer, waiting for a reply, talking into a wooden post that must have a speaker in it.*

**ELAINE** Uh, yes, we're Elaine Lawless and Heather Carver, we have an appointment at one o'clock to talk with a prisoner, Rose Williams.

**VOICE** Say your names again.

*In unison, both women speak their names at once, then realize only one should speak.*

**HEATHER** (*speaking slowly*) Elaine Lawless and Heather Carver. We have an appointment.

*No response. Loud buzzer off to the side. Women stand there a bit perplexed.*

**HEATHER** Oh, I think that means this gate has been unlocked.

*She pushes hesitantly on the iron gate in front of them; it opens with a groan; as soon as she releases it, it clicks back into place. Unconsciously, both women look back at the locked gate behind them.*

**NEW VOICE** (*man's voice from inside booth; his face is not visible*)  Sign in here. Leave everything you are carrying here, including your car keys.

**HEATHER** (*a bit flustered*)  But we have permission to tape-record a prisoner. We need the tape recorder.

**ELAINE**  And I have the extra tapes. Do you want to look at them?

**VOICE**  Yes, slide them under the glass—the tape recorder as well.

*Noises as they hear him opening the tape recorder, removing the tape, looking through the battery case. As their eyes adjust, they can actually see the man, holding the tapes up to the light; they glance at each other with raised eyebrows. They are obviously nervous, uncomfortable.*

**VOICE**  OK. These are clear to go in. Leave the rest of it. You can take in one pad and pen each and the tape recorder and the tapes. Slide everything else under here. Keys, too.

*The women do as instructed. Then they stand nervously waiting for directions. No one says anything. They begin to walk slowly toward the next gate, touching it hesitantly. They are relieved when a woman officer meets them at the gate. She is large, uniformed, and brisk.*

**OFFICER**  Follow me.

*They follow her as they try to also look around them. There are prisoners in gray all over the grass, clipping shrubs, sitting in small groups, pushing wheelbarrows, walking toward other buildings. Officers are everywhere, watching.*

**OFFICER** (*gruffly, as though she's weary and isn't really interested in their answer*)  Have either of you ever been in a prison before?

*Together the women reply, talking over one another.*

**ELAINE AND HEATHER**  Well, I've worked in a women's shelter—
Well, not really, but ah—

*They realize that they are talking over one another again, and both stop.*

**ELAINE**  I've never really been in a prison.

**HEATHER**  No. Unh-uh.

*Officer shrugs a bit, sighs.*

**OFFICER**  OK, here's the drill. You will have to go through the
security monitor separately. I hope you left all your keys and everything else at the front gate. Did you?

*Both women nod vigorously and talk at the same time.*

**ELAINE AND HEATHER**  Yes, yes.

**OFFICER**  OK, well, you walk through this, just like at the airport,
but first give this person here everything you are holding so she can
check it out. Then, sign in here and list everything you are bringing in.

*Officer behind counter looks through the tape recorder, the tapes, the
notepads, replaces their pencils with ballpoint pens.*

**OFFICER**  Now, I need to warn you that you are entering a maxi-
mum security prison. We will walk straight through this common
room where you will see prisoners and some of their relatives who
are visiting them. Don't stop, don't stare, walk quickly. The private
interview rooms are right at the end there, past the machines. Don't
go to the machines. In fact, once you are in the interview room, don't
leave for any reason. I'm going to stand right here, right outside
your room. You'll be able to see me through the glass. You can get
my attention for any reason whatever. Another officer will bring

the prisoner here to you. Remember, you are in a prison setting. You must be aware at all times. These are murderers, remember— criminals. The last thing we need is for one of you to get hurt. Do you understand?

*They follow the officer rather closely and try not to stare at the prisoners and their families spread out over the room talking in low voices, an occasional laugh here, a child cries over there. Mostly it's rather quiet. A really depressing room and scene.*

*They enter the small interview room, where there is only a bare wooden table, oblong, with two chairs on the opposite side, one chair at the forward side.*

**OFFICER** I want you two to sit over here facing the prisoner. When they bring her in, they'll put her in this chair (pulls it out from the table). Now, again, remember, do not touch the prisoner. Call me if you need me.

*Officer leaves the room. The two women look at each other with some surprise and apprehension, leaning toward each other, whispering.*

**ELAINE** Lord—this sounds pretty scary, actually.

**HEATHER** Yeah, what's with the "She's a dangerous criminal" stuff? I've never thought of them that way.

**ELAINE** No kidding. Neither have I.

*They stop abruptly and look up as a large male officer brings in a surprisingly small, frail-looking woman.* ELAINE *and* HEATHER *stare at her a bit as the officer tells her where to sign the forms before she can sit down.*

**OFFICER** How long do you think you'll be in here?

**ELAINE AND HEATHER** (*together, again, talking rather over each other*)

Oh, about an hour . . . or more.

**ELAINE**   Yes, about an hour, or maybe more like two?

**OFFICER**   I'll be right outside the door. Call me if you need me for anything.

*He glances at the prisoner as he walks out the door, closes it behind him, and stands with his back to the glass in the door. A small-framed woman sits quietly in the prisoner chair.* HEATHER *and* ELAINE *take in the hot pink T-shirt under her gray uniform and the many pink, plastic butterflies in her hair. Although her hair is graying, she is really a lovely woman, and the plastic hair barrettes make her look like a whimsical child.*

**ELAINE**   Hello, Rose, thanks for coming. I'm Elaine Lawless, and this is Heather Carver. We've read your story in the clemency files at the university, and, well, we decided we would just like to see you in person, just meet you and hear your story.

**HEATHER**   Yes, we want to hear your story ourselves.

ELAINE *and* HEATHER *move into the audience as* ROSE *begins her story. The lights fade except for a spotlight on* ROSE.
   *She begins.*

# Bibliography

Abu-Lughod, Lila. "Can There Be a Feminist Ethnography?" *Women and Performance: A Journal of Feminist Theory* 5.1 (1990): 7–27.

Allen, Barbara. "Personal Experience Narratives: Use and Meaning in Interaction." *Folklore and Mythology Studies* 2 (1987): 5–7. Rpt. in *Folk Groups and Folklore Genres: A Reader*, ed. Elliott Oring, 236–43. Logan: Utah State University Press, 1989.

Allen, Catherine J., and Garner Nathan. *Condor Qatay: Anthropology in Performance*. Prospect Heights, Ill.: Waveland, 1997.

Allsopp, Ric. "Performance Writing." *PAJ: A Journal of Performance and Art* 21 (January 1999): 76–80.

Anderson, Kristin, and Debra Umberson. "Gendering Violence: Masculinity and Power in Men's Accounts of Domestic Violence." *Gender and Society* 15 (June 2001): 358–80.

Angrosino, Michael V., ed. *Doing Cultural Anthropology*. Prospect Heights, Ill.: Waveland, 2002.

Auslander, Philip. *From Acting to Performance: Essays in Modernism and Postmodernism*. New York: Routledge, 1997.

Bauman, Richard. *Verbal Art as Performance*. Prospect Heights, Ill.: Waveland, 1977.

Behar, Ruth. *The Vulnerable Observer: Anthropology That Breaks Your Heart*. Boston: Beacon, 1996.

Behar, Ruth, and Deborah A. Gordon. *Women Writing Culture*. Los Angeles: University of California Press, 1995.

Benson, Thomas W. "Another Shooting in Cowtown." *Quarterly Journal of Speech* 67 (November 1981): 347–406.

Berger, Peter L., and Thomas Luckmann. *The Social Construction of Reality: A Treatise in the Sociology of Knowledge*. New York: Doubleday Anchor, 1966.

Bochner, Arthur P., and Carolyn Ellis, eds. *Ethnographically Speaking: Autoethnography, Literature, and Aesthetics*. Walnut Creek, Calif.: AltaMira, 2002.

Bonny, Jo, ed. *Extreme Exposure: An Anthology of Solo Performance Texts from the Twentieth Century*. New York: Theatre Communications Group, 2000.

Brown, Karen McCarthy. *Mama Lola: A Vodou Priestess in Brooklyn*. Los Angeles: University of California Press, 2001.

Burgess, Robert G. *Field Research*. London: Allen and Unwin, 1982.

———. *In the Field*. London: Allen and Unwin, 1984.

Burke, Kenneth. *A Grammar of Motives*. Berkeley: University of California Press, 1945.

Burns, Elizabeth. *Theatricality: A Study of Convention in the Theatre and in Social Life*. London: Longman, 1972.

Butler, Judith. *Gender Trouble: Feminism and the Subversion of Identity.* New York: Routledge, 1999.

Carver, M. Heather. "Two Truths and a Lie: Performing Professor/Motherhood." *Journal of American Folklore* 118 (Winter 2005): 78–89.

Carver, M. Heather, and Jeffrey Ullom, eds. *Healthy Primates and Other Plays from the New Play Development Workshop.* Nashville, Tenn.: Association of Theatre in Higher Education, 2004.

Castagno, Paul C. *New Playwriting Strategies: A Language Based Approach to Playwriting.* New York: Routledge, 2001.

Catron, Louis E. *The Elements of Playwriting.* New York: Macmillan, 1993.

Chandler, Sadie Marie. "The First Year: An Autoethnography of the Troubling Violence Performance Project" (Ph.D. dissertation, University of Missouri-Columbia, 2007).

Clifford, James, and George E. Marcus. *Writing Culture: The Poetics and Politics of Ethnography.* Los Angeles: University of California Press, 1986.

Conquergood, Dwight. "Ethnography, Rhetoric, and Performance." *Quarterly Journal of Speech* 78 (1992): 80–123.

———. "Health Theatre in a Hmong Refugee Camp: Performance, Communication, and Culture." *Drama Review* 32 (Autumn 1988): 174–208.

———. "Of Caravans and Carnivals: Performance Studies in Motion." *Drama Review* 39 (Autumn 1995): 137–41.

———. "Performance Studies: Interventions and Radical Research." *Drama Review* 46 (Summer 2002): 145–56.

———. "Performing as a Moral Act." *Literature in Performance* 5 (April 1985): 1–13.

———. "Poetics, Play Process, and Power: The Performative Turn in Anthropology." *Text and Performance Quarterly* 9 (January 1989): 82–88.

———. "Rethinking Ethnography: Towards a Critical Cultural Politics." *Communications Monographs* 59 (June 1991): 179–94.

Corey, Frederick C. "Performing Sexualities in an Irish Pub." *Text and Performance Quarterly* 16 (April 1996): 146–60.

Dailey, Sheron J., ed. *The Future of Performance Studies: Visions and Revisions.* Annandale, Va.: National Communication Association, 1998.

de Caro, Frank. *The Folklore Muse: Poetry Fiction, and Other Reflections by Folklorists.* Logan: Utah State University Press, 2008.

Denzin, Norman K. *Interpretive Ethnography: Ethnographic Practices for the Twenty-first Century.* London: Sage, 1997.

———. "The Many Faces of Emotionality: Reading Persona." In *Investigating Subjectivity,* ed. Carolyn Ellis and Michael Flaherty, 17–30. Newbury Park, Calif.: Sage, 1992.

———. *Performance Ethnography: Critical Pedagogy and the Politics of Culture.* Thousand Oaks, Calif.: Sage, 2003.

Denzin, Norman K., and Yvonna C. Lincoln. *Handbook of Qualitative Research.* Thousand Oaks, Calif.: Sage, 1994.

———. *Strategies of Qualitative Inquiry.* Thousand Oaks, Calif.: Sage, 2003.

Diamond, Elin. *Performance and Cultural Politics.* New York: Routledge, 1996.

———. *Unmaking Mimesis: Essays on Feminism and Theatre.* New York: Routledge, 1997.

Dolan, Jill. *Geographies of Yearning: Theory and Practice, Activism and Performance.* Middleton, Conn.: Wesleyan University Press, 2001.

———. *Presence and Desire: Essays on Gender, Sexuality, Performance.* Ann Arbor: University of Michigan Press, 1993.

Donnell, Alison, and Pauline Polkey, eds. *Representing Lives: Women and Auto/biography.* New York: St. Martin's, 2000.

Edgar, David, ed. *Playwrights on Playwriting.* London: Faber, 1999.

Ellen, R. F., ed. *Ethnographic Research: A Guide to General Conduct.* London: Academic, 1984.

Ellis, Carolyn. *The Ethnographic I: A Methodological Novel about Autoethnography.* Walnut Creek, Calif.: AltaMira, 2004.

Ellis, Carolyn, and Arthur P. Bochner, eds. *Composing Ethnography: Alternative Forms of Qualitative Writing.* Walnut Creek, Calif.: AltaMira, 1996.

Emerson, Robert M., ed. *Contemporary Field Research.* Los Angeles: University of California Press, 2001.

Ensler, Eve. *The Vagina Monologues.* New York: Villard, 2001.

Fine, Elizabeth, and Jean H. Speer, eds. *Performance, Culture, and Identity.* Westport, Conn.: Praeger, 1992.

Fox, Richard. *Recapturing Ethnography: Working in the Present.* Santa Fe, N.M.: School of American Research, 1991.

Fraden, Rena. *Imagining Medea: Rhodessa Jones and Theater for Incarcerated Women.* Chapel Hill: University of North Carolina Press, 2000.

Galloway, Terry, Donna Nudd, and Carrie Sandahl. "Actual Lives and the Ethic of Accommodation." In *Community Performance: A Reader,* ed. Petra Kuppers, 227–34. New York: Routledge, 2007.

Garrison, Gary. *A Playwright's Survival Guide: Keeping the Drama in Your Work and Out of Your Life.* Portsmouth, N.H.: Heinemann, 1999.

Geertz, Clifford. *Interpretation of Culture.* New York: Basic Books, 1977.

———. *Local Knowledge: Further Essays in Interpretive Anthropology.* New York: Basic Books, 1983.

———. *Works and Lives: The Anthropologist as Author.* Stanford, Calif.: Stanford University Press, 1988.

Gingrich-Philbrook, Craig. "Refreshment." *Text and Performance Quarterly* 17 (October 1997): 352–60.

Goffman, Erving. *The Presentation of Self in Everyday Life.* New York: Doubleday Anchor, 1959.

Goodall, H. L. *Writing the New Ethnography.* Walnut Creek, Calif.: AltaMira, 2000.

Hamera, Judith. "The Ambivalent, Knowing Male Body in the Pasadena Dance Theatre." *Text and Performance Quarterly* 14 (1994): 197–209.

Hammersley, Martyn. *What's Wrong with Ethnography?* New York: Routledge, 1992.

Heddon, Deirdre. *Autobiography and Performance.* New York: Macmillan, 2008.

Hemenway, Robert E. *Zora Neale Hurston: A Literary Biography.* Urbana: University of Illinois Press, 1977.

Holman-Jones, Stacy. *Kaleidoscope Notes: Writing Women's Music and Organizational Culture.* Walnut Creek, Calif.: AltaMira, 1998.

Hopper, Robert. "Conversational Dramatism and Everyday Life Performance." *Text and Performance Quarterly* 13 (April 1993): 181–83.

Hughes, Langston, and Zora Neale Hurston. *Mule Bone.* New York: HarperCollins, 1991.

Hurston, Zora Neale. *Go Gator and Muddy the Water.* New York: Norton, 1999.

———. *Jonah's Gourd Vine.* Philadelphia: Lippincott, 1934.

———. *Mules and Men.* Philadelphia: Lippincott, 1935.

———. *Their Eyes Were Watching God.* Philadelphia: Lippincott, 1937.

Huxley, Michael, and Noel Witts, eds. *The Twentieth-Century Performance Reader.* New York: Routledge, 1996.

Hymes, Dell. "Breakthrough into Performance." In *Folklore, Performance and Communication,* ed. Dan Ben Amos and Kenneth Goldstein, 11–75. The Hague: Moutan, 1975.

Jackson, Bruce. *Fieldwork.* Champaign: University of Illinois Press, 1987.

Jackson, Michael. *The Politics of Storytelling: Violence, Transgression, and Intersubjectivity.* Copenhagen: Museum Tusculanum Press, 2002.

Jacobson, David. *Reading Ethnography.* Albany: State University of New York Press, 1991.

Jones, Joni L. "Broken Circles: A Journey through Africa and Self." Unpublished play script, 1994.

———. "Performing Osun without Bodies: Documenting the Osun Festival in Print." *Text and Performance Quarterly* 17 (January 1997): 69–93.

———. "The Self as Other: Creating the Role of Joni the Ethnographer for *Broken Circles.*" *Text and Performance Quarterly* 16 (April 1996): 131–45.

Jones, Stacy Holman. "The Way We Were, Are, and Might Be: Torch Singing as Autoethnography. In *Ethnographically Speaking: Autoethnography, Literature and Aesthetics,* ed. Carolyn Ellis and Arthur Bochner. Walnut Creek, Calif.: AltaMira, 2002.

Kaufman, Moises. *Gross Indecency: The Three Trials of Oscar Wilde.* New York: Vintage, 1998.

Kaufman, Moises, and Members of the Tectonic Theatre Project. *The Laramie Project.* New York: Vintage, 2001.

Kimmel, Michael. Interview. N.d. Available online at www.pbs.org/kued/ nosafeplace/interv/kimmel.html.

Kimmel, Michael. *Manhood in America: A Cultural History.* Oxford: Oxford University Press, 2005.

Kirshenblatt-Gimblett, Barbara. *Destination Culture: Tourism, Museums, and Heritage.* Berkeley: University of California Press.

———. "Objects of Memory: Material Culture as Life Review." In *Folk Groups and Folklore Genres: A Reader,* ed. Elliott Oring, 329–39. Logan: Utah State University Press, 1989.

Kushner, Tony. *Angels in America: A Gay Fantasia on National Themes.* New York: Theatre Communications Group, 2003.

Lather, Patricia Ann. *Troubling the Angels: Women Living with HIV/AIDS.* Boulder, Colo.: Westview, 1997.

Lau, Kimberly. *New Age Capitalism: Making Money East of Eden.* Philadelphia: University of Pennsylvania Press, 2000.

Lawless, Elaine. "'I Was Afraid Someone Like You . . . an Outsider . . . Would Misunderstand': Negotiating Interpretive Differences between Ethnographers and Subjects." *Journal of American Folklore* 105 (Summer 1992): 302–14.

———. *Women Escaping Violence: Empowerment through Narrative.* Columbia: University of Missouri Press, 2001.

Lewis, Barbara. "The Circle of Confusion: A Conversation with Anna Deavere Smith." *Kenyon Review* 15 (Fall 1993): 54–64.

Langellier, Kristin, and Eric Peterson. *Storytelling in Daily Life: Performing Narrative.* Philadelphia: Temple University Press, 2004.

Madison, D. Soyini, and Judith Hamera, eds. *The Sage Handbook of Performance Studies.* Thousand Oaks, Calif.: Sage, 2005.

Mascia-Lees, Frances E., Patricia Sharpe, and Colleen Ballerino Cohen. "The Postmodernist Turn in Anthropology: Cautions from a Feminist Perspective." *Signs* 15 (Autumn 1989): 7–33.

Martin, Carol, interviewer. "Anna Deavere Smith: The Word Becomes You: An Interview." *Drama Review* 37 (Winter 1993): 45–62.

McAuley, Gay. "Towards an Ethnography of Rehearsal." *New Theatre Quarterly* 14 (February 1998): 75–85.

Miller, Lynn C., and Ronald J. Pelias, eds. *The Green Window: Proceedings of the Giant City Conference on Performative Writing.* Carbondale: Southern Illinois University Press, 2001.

Miller, Lynn C., Jacqueline Taylor, and M. Heather Carver, eds. *Voices Made Flesh: Performing Women's Autobiography.* Madison: University of Wisconsin Press, 2003.

Minh-ha, Trinh T. *Woman, Native, Other.* Bloomington: Indiana University Press, 1989.

Myerhoff, Barbara. *Number Our Days.* New York: Simon and Schuster, 1978.

Narayan, Kirin. *Storytellers, Saints, and Scoundrels: Folk Narrative in Hindu Religious Teaching.* Philadelphia: University of Pennsylvania Press, 1989.

Newton, Esther. *Mother Camp: Female Impersonators in America.* Chicago: University of Chicago Press, 1979.

Nudd, Donna Marie, Kristina Schriver, and Terry Galloway. "Is This Theatre Queer?: Mickee Faust and the Performance of Community." In *Performing Community, Performing Democracy: International Perspectives on Urban Community–Based Performance,* ed. Susan C. Haedicke and Tobin Nellhaus, 104–16. Ann Arbor: University of Michigan Press, 2001.

Okely, Judith, and Helen Callaway. *Anthropology and Autobiography.* New York: Routledge, 1992.

Pacanowsky, Michael. "Slouching towards Chicago." *Quarterly Journal of Speech* 74 (November 1988): 453–67.

Packard, William. *The Art of the Playwright: Creating the Magic of Theatre.* New York: Thunder's Mouth, 1997.

Park-Fuller, Linda. "A Clean Breast of It." In *Voices Made Flesh: Performing Women's*

*Autobiography,* ed. Lynn C. Miller, Jacqueline Taylor, and M. Heather Carver, 215–36. Madison: University of Wisconsin Press, 2003.

Parker, Andrew, and Eve Kosofsky Sedgwick, eds. *Performativity and Performance.* New York: Routledge, 1995.

Pelias, Ronald. *A Methodology of the Heart: Evoking Academic and Daily Life.* Walnut Creek, Calif.: AltaMira, 2004.

———. *Writing Performance: Poeticizing the Researcher's Body.* Carbondale: Southern Illinois University Press, 1999.

Perreault, Jeanne Martha. *Writing Selves: Contemporary Feminist Autography.* Minneapolis: University of Minnesota Press, 1995.

Petry, Ann. "Like a Winding Sheet." In *The Miss Muriel and Other Stories,* 111@-24. Boston: Houghton Mifflin, 1999.

Phelan, Peggy. *Unmarked: The Politics of Performance.* New York: Routledge, 1993.

Phelan, Peggy, and Jill Lane. *The Ends of Performance.* New York: New York University Press, 1998.

Pineau, Elyse. "Nursing Mother and Articulating Absence." *Text and Performance Quarterly* 20.1 (2000): 1–19.

"Play." In *Merriam-Webster's Collegiate Dictionary.* Eleventh ed.

Pollock, Della. "A Response to Dwight Conquergood's Essay 'Beyond the Text: Towards a Performative Cultural Politics.'" In *The Future of Performance Studies: Visions and Revisions,* edited by Sheron J. Dailey. Annandale, Va.: National Communication Association, 1998.

———. *Telling Bodies Performing Birth: Everyday Narratives of Childbirth.* New York: Columbia University Press, 1999.

Reason, Peter, and Hilary Bradbury, eds. *Handbook of Action Research: Participative Inquiry and Practice.* Thousand Oaks, Calif.: Sage, 2001.

Redfern-Vance, Nancy. "Analyzing Narrative Data." In *Doing Cultural Anthropology,* edited by Michael V. Angrosino. Prospect Heights, Ill.: Waveland, 2002.

Reed-Danahay, Deborah E., ed. *Auto/Ethnography: Rewriting the Self and the Social.* Oxford: Berg, 1997.

Reinelt, Janelle G., and Joseph R. Roach, eds. *Critical Theory and Performance.* Ann Arbor: University of Michigan Press, 1992.

Richardson, Laurel. *Fields of Play: Constructing an Academic Life.* New Brunswick, N.J.: Rutgers University Press, 1997.

Rosaldo, Renato. *Culture and Truth.* Boston: Beacon, 1993.

Ruby, Jay. *The Crack in the Mirror.* Philadelphia: University of Pennsylvania Press, 1982.

Sawin, Patricia E. "Performance at the Nexus of Gender, Power, and Desire: Reconsidering Bauman's Verbal Art from the Perspective of Gendered Subjectivity as Performance." *Journal of American Folklore* 115 (Winter 2002): 28–61.

Scarry, Elaine. *The Body in Pain: The Making and Unmaking of the World.* New York: Oxford University Press, 1985.

Schechner, Richard. "Anna Deavere Smith: Acting as Incorporation." *Drama Review* 37 (Winter 1993): 63–64.

———. *Between Theatre and Anthropology.* Philadelphia: University of Pennsylvania Press, 1985.

———. *The Future of Ritual: Writings on Culture and Performance.* New York: Routledge, 1993.

Schneider, Rebecca. *The Explicit Body in Performance.* New York: Routledge, 1997.

Shange, Ntozake. *For Colored Girls Who Have Considered Suicide When the Rainbow Is Enuf.* New York: Simon and Schuster, 1997.

Simpson-Stern, Carol, and Bruce Henderson. *Performance Texts and Contexts.* New York: Longman, 1993.

Smith, Anna Deavere. *Fires in the Mirror: Crown Heights, Brooklyn, and Other Identities.* New York: Dramatist Play Service, 1997.

———. *Piano.* New York: Theatre Communications Group, 1989.

———. "Rethinking Power, Rethinking Theatre: A Conversation between Lani Guinier and Anna Deavere Smith." *Theatre* 31 (Fall 2001): 31–45.

———. *Talk to Me: Listening Between the Lines.* New York: Random House, 2000.

———. *Twilight—Los Angeles/1992 on the Road: A Search for American Character.* New York: Anchor, 1994.

Sparkes, Andrew C. "Autoethnography: Self Indulgence or Something More?" In *Ethnographically Speaking: Autoethnography, Literature, and Aesthetics,* ed. Carolyn Ellis and Arthur Bochner, 209–33. Walnut Creek, Calif.: AltaMira, 2002.

Spradley, James P. *The Ethnographic Interview.* New York: Holt, Rinehart, Winston, 1979.

———. *Participant Observation.* New York: Holt, 1980.

Stacey, Judith. "Can There Be a Feminist Ethnography?" *Women's Studies International Forum* 11 (Spring 1988): 21–27.

Stephenson, Heide, and Natasha Langridge. *Rage and Reason: Women Playwrights on Playwriting.* London: Methuen, 1997.

Thompson, Debby. "The Laramie Project (review)." *Theatre Journal* 53 (December 2001): 644–45.

Toelken, Barre. "The Folklore of Academe." In *The Study of American Folklore: An Introduction,* 3rd ed., ed. Jan Harold Brunvand, 317–37. New York: Norton, 1986.

Turner, Victor. *The Anthropology of Performance.* New York: PAJ, 1986.

———. *From Ritual to Theatre.* New York: PAJ, 1982.

Turner, Victor, and Edith Turner. "Performing Ethnography." *Drama Review* 26 (Summer 1982): 33–50.

Vanden Heuvel, Michael. *Performing Drama, Dramatizing Performance: Alternative Theatre and the Dramatic Text.* Ann Arbor: University of Michigan Press, 1991.

Van Italle, Jean Claude. *The Playwright's Workbook.* New York: Applause, 1997.

Visweswaran, Kamala. *Fictions of Feminist Ethnography.* Minneapolis: University of Minnesota Press, 1994.

Weigler, Will. *Strategies for Playbuilding: Helping Groups Translate Issues into Theatre.* Portsmouth, N.H.: Heinemann, 2001.

Wolf, Margery. *A Thrice-Told Tale: Feminism, Postmodernism, and Ethnographic Responsibility.* Stanford, Calif.: Stanford University Press, 1992.

Wolf, Stacy. *A Problem Like Maria: Gender and Sexuality in the American Musical.* Ann Arbor: University of Michigan Press, 2002.

Wright, Michael. *Playwriting in Process: Thinking and Working Theatrically.* Portsmouth, N.H.: Heinemann, 1997.

Yordon, Judy E. *Experimental Theatre: Creating and Staging Texts.* Prospect Heights, Ill.: Waveland, 1997.

CPSIA information can be obtained
at www.ICGtesting.com
Printed in the USA
FFOW01n0747191214
9691FF

9 781604 738698